C-2

C-3

C-4

C-5

C-6

C-8

C-7

C-10

C-11

C-13

C-12

C-14

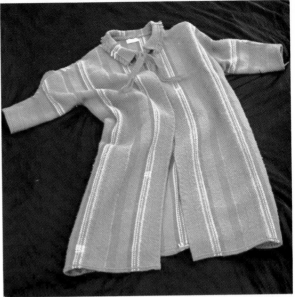

C-15

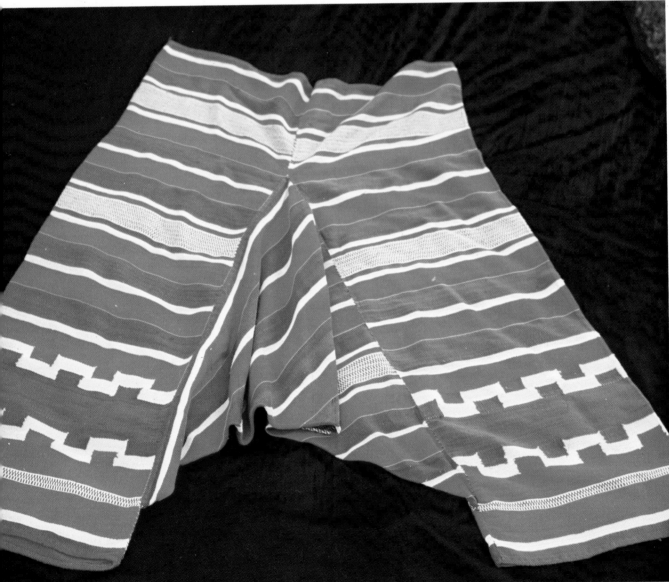

C-16

C-18

C-19

C-20

WEAVING YOU CAN WEAR

JEAN WILSON
WITH JAN BURHEN

15200

VNR VAN NOSTRAND REINHOLD COMPANY
NEW YORK   CINCINNATI   TORONTO   LONDON   MELBOURNE

Only with the enthused and generous cooperation of these people was it possible to put this book together—and my very grateful thanks to all of them:

Jan Burhen, who wove and sewed and figured directions—and modeled her lovely clothes. My daughter-in-law, Sheri Wilson, who modeled so beautifully. My son, Gary Wilson, who ably did all of the drawings. Kent Kammerer, who again expertly and patiently photographed clothes, people, and animal! Beverly Rush, who photographed with skill and interest. Nancy Newman, who urged me to do the book. Luana Sever, who continually weaves exciting, new, and different concepts in sophisticated techniques—and always willingly shares them in my books. Special thanks to Del O'Neill and Bob Cobb for the joy of working and playing with Guanama Llama. And, certainly, to all of you who let us photograph your handsome handwovens.

Van Nostrand Reinhold Company Regional Offices:
New York Cincinnati Chicago Millbrae Dallas

Van Nostrand Reinhold Company International Offices:
London Toronto Melbourne

Copyright (c) 1973 by Litton Educational Publishing, Inc.
Library of Congress Catalog Card Number 73-1634
ISBN 0-442-29514-6 (paper)
ISBN 0-442-29511-1 (cloth)

All drawings of patterns and plans by Gary Wilson

Published by Van Nostrand Reinhold Company
450 West 33rd Street, New York, N.Y. 10001

16   15   14   13   12   11   10   9   8   7   6   5   4   3   2

C-1. Huichol Indian man, Mexico, wearing his pocket belt over other belts, with two shoulder bags, all on his beautifully embroidered trousers and long shirt. His companions are Huichol, too, and the lady is wearing a special quechquemitl made to wear on the head.

C-2. A group of *huipiles*, assembled from three rectangles. All are from the state of Oaxaca, but each one is of a distinctive and different design, by five separate Indian groups.

C-3. A Mixtec man (Tacuate) from the state of Oaxaca wears his extraordinary costume in a unique manner: full trousers, rolled up at the waist—very short; open-sided shirt, of two long rectangles, bound around with a wide, long belt; the yard-long front and back ends of the shirt are pulled up and tucked into the belt, making a convenient carrying pocket. All finely embroidered. Behind him, the very long, light panel is one of the belts, more than 12″ wide, several yards long. The small dark rectangle is a child's serape.

C-4. Detail of a Huichol Indian pocket belt.

C-1 through C-4: all from an exhibition of Mexican costumes and objects from the collection of Fred and Leslie McCune Hart, La Tienda, Seattle. Shown at the Friends of the Crafts Gallery, Seattle. (Photographs by Paul Macapia)

C-5. *Huipil*-into-jacket. Adapted by author. (Photograph by Kent Kammerer)

C-6. Elaborately draped sari. Photographed in India, by Frances Sharpe.

C-7. Wool "Put-over," of two rectangles. By author. (Photograph by Beverly Rush)

C-8. A Portugese shepherd in his sheepskin coat. (Photograph by Frances Sharpe)

C-9. Sherpa coat, all from fourteen-inch-wide fabric. Weaver, Jan Burhen. (Photograph by Kent Kammerer)

C-10. Long tunic, with slit-weave panels. Woven by Judy Thomas. (Photograph by Paul Thomas)

C-11. Shaped après-ski poncho, handspun wool. Woven by Sylvia Tacker. (Photograph by Beverly Rush)

C-12. Inside view of fur and wool quechquemitl, double-weave. By Hope Munn. Shown courtesy of Nancy Ewell. (Photograph by Beverly Rush)

C-13. Long skirt, tubular weave with tapestry-weave pattern. Woven by Judy Thomas. (Photograph by Paul Thomas)

C-14. Tunic. Note the neckline, which follows the lines of the fabric pattern, and the covered buttons. By Jan Burhen. (Photograph by Kent Kammerer)

C-15. Brushed-wool coat. By author. (Photograph by Kent Kammerer)

C-16. African pants, of two rectangles and a square. Courtesy, Mr. and Mrs. Fred Hart. (Photograph by Kent Kammerer)

C-17. The Kbee Koat. By Jan Burhen. (Photograph by Kent Kammerer)

C-18. "Blue Rainbirds," umbrella of leather and wool tapestry-weave. By Luana Sever. (Photograph by Beverly Rush)

C-19. Open-weave parasol. By Luana Sever. (Photograph by Beverly Rush)

C-20. Cape, of leather and wool. By Luana Sever. (Photograph by Beverly Rush)

Front cover: Guanama, the llama; the Burhenoose, and Jan. O'Neill and Bob Cobb, Vashon Island, Washington, own two llamas which they hire out as pack animals, and take walking every night. This is what they say of these charming beasts: very versatile pets for anyone with grazing land; beasts of burden; source of wool and hides; loyal companions; friendly with children.
The most fun of all in putting this book together was photographing this friendly creature. His companion, however, would have nothing to do with us, and kept a distance! (Photograph by Kent Kammerer)

CONTENTS

FOREWORD

This book is on how to weave and use hand-woven coverings for people and how to weave for special effects and fitting by shaping and combining woven units for clothing. The premise is that everything that comes off a loom is basically a square or a rectangle because the construction is threads at right angles. Variations come in a necessarily rounded corner, a slit, and the combining of different units or shapes. Primitive looms were usually limited in size, so long rectangles and squares were woven and pieced together to make body coverings of larger size, attached sleeves, and so on. Because we feel deeply that what craftsmen did before is very important to us now, we make a deep bow to the primitive weavers of the world who were so inventive and productive. Our necessarily brief scan hardly touches on the material available for study, but it may send you off on a search that you had not thought about. Note that many of the weaves are loom-patterned. An interesting phase of the design of clothing made up of rectangles and small units is planning and weaving stripes, or allover patterns; placing bands or areas of pattern weaving; weaving one color in pattern for a subtle pattern-texture. Using every technique available to a weaver means loom-pattern, weaver-controlled weaves such as laid-in, tapestry, loops, double and tubular weaves,

and the ways of joining and embellishing with needle and yarn.

Except for clothing or other articles that are shaped on the loom during the weaving process, all of these ideas can be made up in handwoven yardage or in commercial fabrics. The non-weaver can purchase suitable yardage and achieve the look of these when there is no way of having them woven. The same shapes of the handwoven pieces can be used by cutting and finishing them.

Placing these coverings into orderly groups was sometimes difficult—and always a bit baffling! All can be woven in separate pieces to exact size and then assembled. Some are woven with warp added or subtracted to achieve a special shape. We mention alternate ways of weaving and assembling to give a choice. The placement of garments in the book is generally decided by the shape of the major part of the garment. Divisions are those made from a single rectangle, two rectangles, two rectangles with additions, and so on. Cut and sew, tubular weave, and loom-shaped are other groups. How to weave slits, neck openings, and shaped pieces is detailed only once—in the loom-shaped section—but most of those in the rectangles section use one or more of these weaving techniques. For clothing, we include decorative or plain joinings, closures, finishes, trims, along with accessories such as handbags, belts, collars, pockets—and umbrellas!

The use of this book is universal, but it is written as a weaving book. It tells how to weave specialized fabrics and what to do with handwoven textiles to provide coverings for people.

I am much indebted to Jan Burhen for the meticulous directions, dimensions, assembling and finishing details for the garments presented in depth and those shown in small drawings. Her experience, interest, and research on these styles based on primitive looms and coverings have been invaluable. We share a deep regard for early weavers and their efforts, skill, and ingenuity. It has been a pleasure to discuss, plan, and work out this part of the book with her.

Jean Wilson

Jean Wilson and I have always shared an interest in garments that were simple in design, of ethnic origin, and unique in their loom control development. To me the challenge has been to think in simple squares and rectangles that the loom produces and to fashion these into wearables with as little adaptation as possible, letting the mind run free and seeing the shapes join for uncluttered simplicity. My most free experience was in the "building" of the Burhenoose. This process seems to me to be the way that primitive peoples developed their coverings of joined rectangle-type garments.

The intrigue of planning design, stripes, color, and texture was a further creative experience. I hope you will be caught up in this simple and dimensional approach to garment designing and making. It provides a joy in searching the origin of man's clothing design and thinking in the untold possibilities of the art of weaving.

Jan Burhen

INTRODUCTION

The enrichment of our surroundings is served by handcrafting textiles to use and wear in our daily lives. Techniques and methods suggest ideas for weaving even though we no longer *need* to weave fabrics for clothing or household use. Like the well-worn saying that sawing your own firewood warms you twice, so does the act of weaving a textile give you pleasure over and over. Designing and planning; putting materials and tools together to weave your cloth; shaping; fabricating; finishing; then wearing or using, all add up to a continuing pleasant experience. Unlike the firewood, textiles last and last, to warm body and soul time and again. There is such logic and satisfaction in weaving a textile for a particular purpose. The loom, yarns, colors, and methods are carefully planned so that the finished cloth will be just right. Special subtle shaping, or sizing, is done for a minimum of cutting, fitting, and sewing. A jacket can be woven with neckline and sleeves carefully shaped on the loom, or a dress woven to your own dimensions.

So here is a collection of ways that weavers of today, primitive peoples, and those in between have used. The book is not intended to be a copybook, or to imply that there is only one way to fill a textile need, but to show possible ways to solve and weave for special textile needs. Perhaps our thinking about weaving, shaping, fitting, and sewing will guide you to a new approach to clothing fabrication.

A book such as this contributes to hand weavers of clothing not just another pattern book, but it shows sound historical and ethnic bases for the garments. The first question: What can the loom plus a weaver do to make a textile conform to the rounded human body? Combining rectangles and squares, with some loom-shaping, and making adaptations and abundant variations may be far-out, or very practical and conservative. While basically classic and enduring, these styles can be made contemporary by stylish use of color and yarns and by the manner worn.

Our goal is to spark your creative imagination. It is to help you develop your inventive approach—especially to the process of garment construction—by working with basic rectangles as the pattern.

1

ETHNIC BODY COVERINGS

Our definition of primitive body coverings is this: Basic; simple; design evolving from the size of the loom, materials at hand, and need; ethnic patterns, shapes, and uses.

The world is full of picturesque regional clothing. Museums abound with primitive looms, tools, and body coverings. Primitive looms produced remarkably sophisticated weavings in the hands of early designer-weavers. Some of our everyday wearables come directly from these sources —shawls, ponchos, tunics, easy-fitting coats and jackets. This book only hints at the rich sources for patterns, colors, textures, and methods. Search for others. You will be well rewarded.

Primitive weavers met their needs for body coverings with available materials and tools. Their inborn talent for good, basic design is evident in the carefully crafted textiles, as well as in the tools they devised to produce them.

Form follows function, and, just as surely, the tool influences the look of the product. A primitive loom does not produce as machine-perfect a fabric or as great a quantity as a power loom. Because of the limitations and characteristics of a simple tool, a whole new approach to design, to technique, and to ways of working is required. We have to go back a bit and work at achieving the simple beauty of fabrics from a simple loom, accustomed as we are to modern production tools. The basic method and loom construction have hardly changed from the beginning! Modern weavers can simulate early weavings, and a very real challenge it is. There is a charm and inherent beauty in primitive fabrics.

DEVELOPMENT OF CLOTHING DESIGN

Loom size, plus human size, plus amount of body area to be covered all contributed to the development of clothing designs. Further development evolved from man's need to embellish and ornament the product: to spend much time and loving effort in the hand-fashioning; and to create something beautiful to his eyes and a joy to use, or wear.

A breechcloth could cover, whether plain or fancy, but there are elaborate examples of those woven, printed, embroidered, or beaded. Some of them are astonishing in their sophisticated technique.

A plain cord or band of cloth could serve as a sash or girdle, but some of the most ornate textile treasures made were for this purpose. Loin skirts and girdles with long beaded panels of the early dynasties of Egypt contributed to the later royal aprons and skirts.

The banded trimmings on Coptic tunics—*clavi* and roundels and the shape of the dalmatic with *clavi*, a loose, tunic-like outer garment—survive today in church vestments. Tracing shapes, uses, and ornamentation on clothing, recognizing bits and pieces of these ancient cultures in what we wear today is a fascinating study.

Narrow looms, plus the need for wide robes, led to the methods of joining small units. The 6″ strips of Kente cloth, woven in Ghana, are joined into enveloping robes. The 12″ strips woven on looms in Nepal led to the distinctive construction of the

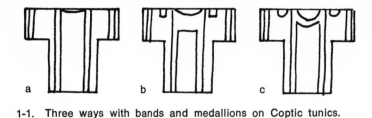

1-1. Three ways with bands and medallions on Coptic tunics.

1-2. Offcenter neckline from Burma.

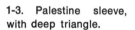

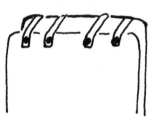

1-3. Palestine sleeve, with deep triangle.

1-4. Shoulder closure from Greek chiton. Use on the Harem Gown.

1-5. Kurdish coat sleeve. Fur on the inside, sleeve loose.

Sherpa coat. Conversely, the need for a wide, flowing garment sometimes led to the building of a wide loom. Coptic tunics were presumably woven on wide, vertical looms. Evidence is found in carvings and paintings of ingenious looms—vertical and horizontal.

The development of these simple body coverings to conform to our lives of today affords some interesting comparisons. We now tend to borrow from—but modify—all primitive styles. For comfort and mobility we tend to cut down on width, length, corners, and the bulk of extra cloth. Instead of weaving an extra yard or two and tucking it into a girdle, we favor weaving a shorter length, adding the girdle, and making a more practical garment. The emphasis these days on leisure, at-home time, and high-fashion costumes has brought many of the long, flowing styles to the fore—the harem dress, burnoose, caftan, and capes.

Emphasis on individuality also has given craftsmen more courage to design, weave, and wear colorful ethnic-source apparel. The beauty of these simple styles is evident in those we bring you here. They can be woven and shaped, of natural colors and simple details, to fit into the most conservative of wardrobes. They can be woven of wildly bright, textured yarns, flamboyantly fringed and trimmed to suit free souls. This, too, is all part of the whole joy of exploring the fashioning of body coverings.

Brief Mention

In Guatemala, a clever folding of long lengths of fabric makes usable units. Folded squares serve as headgear and as slings for baby-carriers or other commodities. Coiled on the head, they serve as pads for carrying baskets or pots.

In Mexico, squares carry candles to church, tortillas to market, hold any small treasures, top a basket, or are worn as head cloths.

We may think the layered look a 1970s' invention, but look at Tibet. Short-sleeved tunics are worn with long-sleeved shirts underneath. Aprons, sashes, and sleeveless vests top these garments.

In ancient Greece and Rome, placement of the

1-6. Spanish collar—a square with diagonal opening.

1-7. Shape for a cape—from an old European painting.

1-8. Use of stripes and triangles, in an African shirt.

1-9. Otomi, Mexico, upper garment. Wide rectangle with wide stripes, sewn front and back to two rectangles, with narrow stripes. Two vertical rectangles are sewn together a few inches, front and back, leaving a deep neck slit front and back. It just reaches the waist, and is worn with a blouse underneath. (Notebook sketches, by author.)

girdle denoted status. Neatness of the tying of a girdle and distribution of the folds was a character clue.

In cold countries, pile weaves give added warmth; they simulate animal skins.

In warm countries, fabrics are airy and clothing easy fitting.

Indians use fringes to add movement in dancing, and to give an attractive finish to leather edges.

Northwest Indians made raincapes of softened inside cedar bark, and wide hats of cedar root—a neat use of indigenous material.

Pockets developed as useful carriers that were a part of the garment. Some became purely decorative and were not placed, or sized, for use.

Waist robes and capes are sometimes worn interchangeably, as skirts, aprons, or shoulder coverings.

Multiple-use coverings are many. A *casula* (little house) is a poncho-like slipover, wide and long, used as cloak or tent. It evolved into the chasuble of church vestments. One, two, or three rectangles, seamed but unfitted, can be used as a shawl, or as a bed-covering. And so on!

BORROWING IDEAS

The informal sketches in this section show some of the details and ideas we have run across in our pursuit of clothing development. You might find a place for these intriguing ideas or they might help you find a solution to a design problem. Some adaptations are noted, too, as they occurred to us. You will think of others. (See Figures 1–1 through 1–9.)

Coptic Tunics

A fine weaving project, which could be a real work of art, is the fashioning of a tunic after the beautifully detailed Coptic tunics. This intriguing source reaches back to the fourth century. A study of these earliest Egyptian Christians—their craftwork, religion, and customs—is all intertwined with the exquisitely detailed weavings which we can study in museum collections. Sketches and

suggestions merely hint at tunic patterns and weaving details. Evidence has been found of weaving centers, hired weavers, guilds, official and peasant art, a linen center, tools, and wide vertical looms. There is proof that the garments were woven on looms wide enough for the length, with the weft running vertically when the garment was worn.

A neck opening, or slit, was woven into the garment. Medallions, bands, yokes, roundels, and other shapes were added for decoration, or to denote status. Necklines were varied, and length and placement of the bands were changeable. The ornamental shapes were usually woven as a part of the plain linen garment as tapestry-weave inserts. However, because of their infinite detail and pictorial beauty, they were cut from worn tunics and applied to new ones. Therefore, they became appliqués, or insets, probably serving as decoration on many garments in succession. These fragments are among the preserved ones for us to see and study. Modern weavers can take these historical examples and apply the ideas today. Perhaps for the sake of preserving your finely woven medallion or band, it would be wise to weave it separately and apply it to the tunic or shirt. This is particularly so in our day of constant fashion change. But the challenge of weaving a whole garment, with woven-in tapestry details, is one for a true designer-craftsman to explore. It is well worth a try.

North African Man's Pants

With singing colors—red, yellow, and blue —varied stripes, and a band of plain-weave tapestry, these pants, woven of very fine soft cotton, have a lot going for them. They provide a number of good ideas to adapt for a lady's version! The method of weaving and assembling them is discussed on page 75. The pants are shown in Figures 1–10, 3–77, and C–16.

To adapt, weave in a cotton or very fine wool that will drape and not be bulky. Pattern, stripes, patterned bands, several sizes of yarn, and many colors will all be suitable for these gala britches. The center square can be modified to suit your size and the fabric. The waistline can be made adjustable by sewing in a drawstring tube, tapering the side seams, or putting in a few darts. Have fun wearing these pants at parties at home or away!

African Shirt or Tunic

An interesting use of stripes appears in this man's shirt from northern Ghana (Figure 1–11). The sleeves are set deep into the shirt so that the stripes become a design element. Inset triangles also provide a slight flare, an idea for skirts or shirts. (See Figure 3–33 and page 48.) The characteristic machine-stitched designs around the necklines of most African garments can be emulated with hand-work or machines in many colors, as they do.

1-12. Black silk man's kimono, from Japan.

1-13. To show the printed silk lining, and the rectangular shapes. Courtesy, Ron Wilson. (Photographs by Beverly Rush)

1-14. Northwest Coast Indian waist robe or dance apron. From the Rasmussen Collection, Portland Art Museum, Portland, Oregon.

A Man's Japanese Kimono
Of black silk, beautifully sewn by hand, completely lined, with a panel of subtly patterned silk inside, this kimono yields a wealth of inspiration for fashioning a coat from rectangles. Slight easement is achieved by a narrow triangle inset in the sides (see detail, Figure 3–33). The tie closure is a tightly plaited cord of silk. Instead of the family crest, a small monogram might be worked at the shoulder, or in the center back just beneath the collar. The long, narrow strip up the front and around the neck is a good detail. It could be woven in a pattern or contrast. The deep rectangular sleeves could be modified somewhat.

Northwest Indian Waist Robe
Fringes, bangles and beads, leather, and flannel ornament the leather dance apron, or waist robe (Figure 1–14). It suggests the possibilities of weaving a similar one for a peplum, decorative apron, or an apron/cape. Adapt it for the top of a long skirt, or a very wide girdle. Make it a rectangle, or shape it at top or bottom. Add woven or knotted ties, warp fringes, bands or woven tabs, beaded or knotted fringe.

Servilleta
An idea for a brocade-weave informal carryall or a scarf is shown in Figure 1–15. It gives a detail of the typical animal and bird motifs woven into *servilleta* cloths by the women of the Huave group in the state of Oaxaca, Mexico. This one is all purple on white cotton. Purple dyes are extracted from certain shellfish, and this color is identified with these weavers. The women use these cloths to wrap tortillas, carry treasures, or sometimes fold them as head coverings.

1-15. *Servilleta* from the state of Oaxaca, Mexico.
Courtesy Mr. and Mrs. Fred Hart, La Tienda, Seattle.
(Photograph by Kent Kammerer)

16

2

GENERAL SPECIFICATIONS

Refer to these general notes on procedures *before* beginning to weave, or to assemble, a garment. Read them over before planning. These directions apply to certain steps to take on each project and to special situations. They will not be repeated in the specific directions.

DIMENSIONS

Pattern Key

Here is how to determine the basic dimensions for all garments. More specific details and directions are given for each garment where necessary.

Sizing

In sizing primitive, or simple, rectangular garments, the following measurements must be taken into consideration:

Length of garment from shoulder to desired hem length

Width between shoulder crests

Hip width about 8″ below waist

Desired sleeve length from joining place at shoulder, or from neck in some garments

Neck openings

Measurements

Following are some of the measurements we have found to work best for some of the items listed above. These apply to a medium size (12–14) throughout. Variations may be made for your own needs and preferences, but this proportioning is most effective.

Body of Garment

Length: Your choice.

Width: 14″, finished, for the rectangle that forms the center of a garment; for example, T-tunics, rectangles with sleeve and side additions. This width is also ideal for the sleeve rectangles and splitting for side vents. Allow for ample seams and weaving take-up, and provide adequate hip room.

Neck Openings

Width: The optimum width seems to be 5½″ to 6″. This prevents any pulling away at the shoulders.

Back: 1″ to 1½″ from top of shoulder after folding material in half.

Front: Front of neck openings can be varied according to your imagination and dictates of the cloth—stripes, plaid, or pattern. In general, the lowest point should be no more than 8″ below the top center fold. A most helpful way to develop neck opening shapes, and a way to try them on, is found in Figure 4–11.

The procedure for marking openings—neck, sleeve, and vents—is as follows:

Fold material length in half.

Fold material width in half.

Mark center with large pin. Work from pin to obtain measurements.

Sleeve Width and Armhole Opening

For most garments, the best width for the sleeve is 8″ to 10″ finished.

Length of sleeve will depend entirely on your own size and comfort.

The size of the armhole opening is also based on your measurements, ease, style of garment, and proportion.

Note: In changing sizes from those noted in the pattern sections, be aware of the proportions of the garment. Some dimensions may be changed, while others are best left the same. For example, the width of a center rectangle may be widened by 2″, while sleeve dimensions remain as indicated for the proper proportioning. This will be readily determined if you draw a plan of the garment on paper, then measure yourself, and work out the necessary dimensions. One further safe step is to make a newspaper or cloth pattern to check proportions and fit. These garments fit casually, but some dimensions, such as hip and bust, are critical.

To Weave

Selection of Yarn

Yarn and finished fabric weight is entirely up to the weaver. Many of these simple styles are most successful when a fairly sizable hand-spun or plied wool is used. Softspun, or a combination of a hard twist and soft, is sometimes desirable. However, these styles lend themselves to almost any fabric that is firmly woven and has some character. Choose cotton, linen, wool, silk, or synthetic yarns. For example: for a reversible burnoose, you might choose a lofty wool for one side and a fine wool or silk for the reverse. All usual rules and good sense about clothing fabrics apply—perhaps even more than in a conventional cut and sewn pattern—because the fabric itself is such an important part of the whole design and style.

Sett

The term "sett" indicates the number of warps per inch. It will, of course, depend upon your yarn, weight of fabric desired, and the plan. We have not included this in our weaving directions because it is a variable.

Weaving Take-up

We have mentioned take-up in some of our directions but, generally speaking, this depends upon the weaver. You may have a beat and a weaving rhythm that takes up more or less than another weaver using the same yarn and sett. A good idea—especially if you are in doubt—is always to make a sample of the fabric and note the take-up in warp and weft—selvedge to selvedge. Also test the shrinkage.

Warp Length

To determine warp length, all parts of the garment must be taken into consideration—body, sleeves, side additions, fringe, or hem allowance—and the total inches added up. Draw the pattern out on paper for a more visual dimensioning.

Refer to Figure 2–1 for a typical process of determining the length of the warp, and to the following explanation. This is for a sleeved tunic, as in Figures 3–29 and 3–30.

28″ front
28″ back
32″ two sleeves
20″ for sides
10″ allowance for fringe and hems

118″ total length

Remember to add additional warp length for tie-in, take-up, shrinkage, and sampling.

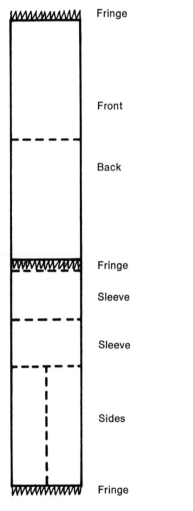

Fringe

Front

Back

Fringe

Sleeve

Sleeve

Sides

Fringe

2-1. Typical plan for dimensions.

Weaving Slits and Shaping Necklines
Detailed instructions on these loom procedures are in the loom-shaping section. Following are a few general suggestions:

When necklines are fashioned on the loom, the warp ends left unwoven must be darned back into the cloth. Sometimes this is best done on the loom while the warp is in tension. A cautious idea is to cut a few, darn in, cut, darn, and so on.

There is also another way to dispose of the warp ends. After cutting the warp ends, draw them through the fabric to the top side, ½" or more down from the last row of weaving. This can be done by threading them into a blunt needle or catching them with a crochet hook. They can be knotted in groups, with ends left as fringe, which provides a different, integral trim. If ends are long, they can be couched, twisted, braided, or otherwise manipulated into a border trim. This is a good way to shape a neckline slightly in a shallow curve, rolling the last rows of weaving over into a hem. It is also a good way to shape a straight shawl at the back of the neck.

Hems
Usually—and preferably—all hem ends will be finished in the weaving process. They will be a selvedge, an allowance woven, or extra warp left for fringe. The finishing of hem ends is then purely a design project. You will decide whether to turn them back and hand sew them; leave as a selvedge; knot a simple, or elaborate, fringe; or make a feature of them by adding embroidery stitches or bands.

Seams

One suggestion that you will find repeated time and again is that a decorative stitch will be appropriate as a joining, or to feature some of the seams. Adding these touches is what makes your garment distinctive, a truly handcrafted, individually designed project. So, within the limits of good design, good taste, and suitability for the particular garment, try to finish everything by hand. Many times, for strength and durability, machine seaming is necessary, but if this is obvious, at least run a thread through it by hand, which gives it the special line of threaded running stitch.

Closures

Your ingenuity and design prowess are really challenged by closures. Usually, the garment will suggest the type and material most suitable for the fastening—leather thongs, plaited cords, hooks, clasps, pins, bone buttons. Just be sure that it is in character with the fabric and garment. Suggestions on pages 115-18, as well as photographs of clothing, provide some views of those we think are right. For instance, we hope you would never fasten a Kbee Koat of homespun wool with an elaborate rhinestone brooch! Or close a finely woven silk with heavy bone buttons! Sometimes the pattern weave of a fabric will suggest the shaping of a neckline (see Figure C–14), or the best ornament. When patterns evolve from the richness of nature's fibers, hand-crafted procedures, and primitive needs for covering, your choices of added material should come from nature: wood, bone, leather, and yarns.

Go-withs

As to what to wear over, on, or with your hand-fashioned garments, here are a few suggestions: Usually, a neutral, low-key plain under-dress or shirt and pants should be chosen. Your prideful production is the star. Don't spoil the effect with the wrong color, texture, or type of accessory and under-dress. While ponchos, capes, and jackets are ideal to fling on and use for casual cover-ups, still you should give some thought to the total effect.

DEFINITIONS

Certain terms used in this text are defined here.
Additions: Pieces added on, or inset, for easement or enlargement.
Finished width, finished length: The dimension, after the garment is seamed and the hem ends completed.
Flat-needle joining, or flat-join: Edge just meeting edge and hand-sewn together.
Loom-shaped: A section of the garment, such as an armhole, woven in the shape needed, to the correct size, with selvedge sides, and requiring no cutting; also, a whole garment woven in the pattern shape, or additions woven to shape, as a triangle.

RL, RLs: Abbreviation for rectangle, rectangles, used in specific directions for brevity.

Seam: Two edges sewn together—selvedge to selvedge with no overlap; or a conventional seam where two pieces are put together and stitched on the machine.

Sew: Sew by hand, with needle and thread. On handwovens, we always mean using the same yarn as in the weave, or a matching one. Where it is necessary to use a sewing thread, match carefully so that it will be invisible.

Slit-weave: Plain-weave tapestry technique —Kelim: weaving with two shuttles, meeting and returning around adjacent warps, leaving a space or slit; procedure used when leaving a neck slit, vents, buttonholes, or a front opening.

Stitch: Sew by machine.

Stitched-seam or joining: Two pieces stitched together in the usual seaming found on all conventionally sewn garments.

Vent: An opening, or slit, for easy entry or easement.

CODE USED IN DIAGRAMS

The following code has been devised to simplify the understanding of the construction diagrams:

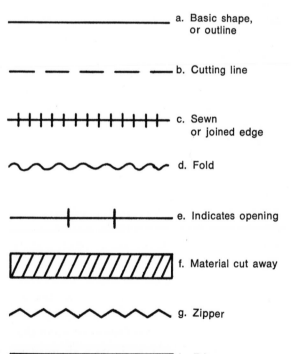

2-2. Code used on diagrams.

Note: Unless otherwise shown or mentioned, garments are the same front and back.

3

HANDWOVEN COVERINGS FOR PEOPLE

3-1. Basic shapes.

Our selection of handwoven clothing is strongly rooted in primitive body coverings, but developed and refined for our day. We show you wide choices in methods, yarns and styles, weights and patterns in the fabrics. We think you will find some that are "you." We *know* there are many to challenge your interest, imagination, and talent.

Which came first—the rectangle produced by the loom, or the need to devise garments? The fascinating fact is that looms do produce rectangles and that rectangles can be made into handsome and functional garments—an endless creative process.

Looms of history have produced rectangles and squares of various sizes. The backstrap loom produces long, narrow rectangles. Vertical looms produce units of varying dimension. When taken from the loom as completed cloth, these lengths challenge the ingenuity of the clothing designer to develop them into coverings for the human form.

Man needed large protective coverings. He wrapped his woven rectangles about him as a

cloak; joined small units for a larger size, and sometimes he left an opening for his head for an even more comfortable garment.

A covering was needed for the upper part of the body that allowed freedom of arm movement and protection from the elements. Shirts and blouses were constructed from the basic rectangle and additional strips of various sizes were added for sleeves; short to long, narrow or wide, depending on need and sense of ornamentation.

Lower body coverings evolved from simple rectangles which formed the early-day loincloth, to one rectangle gathered into a skirt and two rectangles joined for pants.

Head coverings, sashes, belts, carrying bags, and many other accessories and adornments were also fashioned from the basic shapes woven on looms.

We have chosen to describe ways of weaving and making clothing that are based on these simple, classic methods of shaping and putting cloth together with a minimum of cutting, sewing, and fitting. These ways have been used for hundreds

of years. All are drawn from ethnic sources such as the Coptic tunic, Mexican *huipil,* Himalayan Sherpa coat, African shirts, South American ponchos—and more. Where possible, we mention, or illustrate the ethnic source. The original ones are numerous and exciting and lend themselves perfectly to modern adaptation.

Versatility in handwoven garments can be achieved by weaving them on a narrow loom and assembling the sections, or weaving them on a wide loom with less joining. Sections and details can be woven in, such as a shaped armhole, neck opening, and slits for belts. Stripes and woven bands can be integrated and placed just where the design requires. Most of the first coverings were woven on small looms such as backstrap and warp-weighted looms, or possibly on small frame looms. These patterns have developed from the size of the weaving equipment, with the resultant textiles constructed to fit the body.

There are two distinct construction methods to follow:
Basic rectangles/squares; assembling woven units

Shaping techniques on the loom; special treatment during the weaving, such as shaping, openings, integral trims, and so on.

Following is an overview of the two methods.

Basic rectangles/squares: How to plan, weave, assemble, and finish the garment.

Shaping techniques on the loom: How to shape the separate sections; how to weave details for ornamentation, joinings, or hems; how to finish, to make each garment individual.

3-3.

ONE RECTANGLE—LONG, NARROW

The simplest of all body coverings is made from a single, long rectangle, which is draped, wrapped, or otherwise arranged. It may be a skirt, a top, or a whole garment. The Indian sari—yards long—is graceful wrapped and draped to form bodice and skirt (Figure 3–2).

23

3-4. Shawl—*rebozo*—from Mexico. This one is wool, all golden yellow, with macramé fringe. From La Tienda, Seattle. (Photograph by Kent Kammerer)

The Mexican rebozo (shawl) is often deeply fringed with elaborate knotted warp ends or macramé open patterns. Sometimes there is more trim than woven fabric (Figure 3–4). Added decoration may take the form of warp patterns —stripes, plaids, brocade, or tapestry. Versions of single rectangles as coverings are found in such diverse fabrics as the heavy wool shawls of Ireland, the cool cotton sarongs of the tropics, and sheer saris and shawls from India.

A long, narrow length of cloth becomes a scarf, stole, or simple tunic. The unshaped length wraps about neck and shoulders. It can be draped over one shoulder and held with a fastener such as the Scottish plaid; flung around the shoulders and hugged in. Or a slit or hole can be cut into the center for the head so it becomes a simple shirt. The sides can be fastened with lacings, an arrangement such as cufflinks, snaps, or buttons, or can be held in place with belt or sash. More refinements come with some side seaming and cutting to form a loose sleeve.

Coverings with the neck openings, slits for a belt, buttonholes, or trims as an integral part of the whole weaving process follow. Directions for weaving the details of shaped necklines, arm slits, vents, and so on are in the section on loom-shaping.

Tunic or Tabard

The tabard is a simple covering that originated with the Roman tunics made from one rectangle. It usually reaches to the widest hip measurement, but it can be made any length desired. The seams are sewn at the sides. Large armholes are left and seams are open at the hem. Diversity and creativity are the keys to this garment, as can be seen in our photographed examples.

General directions follow.

Dimensions
Length: Your measured length, plus loom tie-in and take-up allowance.
Width: 20″ in the loom for medium size.

To Weave
The neck slit is woven 6″ to 8″ wide. The front slit is woven with two shuttles to about 8″. Any other openings, such as slits for a belt, are fashioned on the loom. (See loom-shaping, page 90.)

To Assemble
The sides are joined with a plain seam or a decorative joining. Ties or loops can be woven in, or added later, if this closure is preferred to a long seam.

Two Tabards with Different Details
Phyllis Kessel likes to solve many weaving problems in each project, and every one of her handsome, wearable weavings is an interesting study in techniques. She has woven for her own wardrobe a number of tabards, other toppers, and accessories. Each problem is solved as part of her learning, resulting in a group of lovely garments, handbags, and belts.

The wide rectangular neck opening of the black wool tabard is woven in (Figure 3-5). A bright wool laid-in design—alternating Os in hot pink and gold—enhances and enlivens the plain-weave black wool. A braided cord with tasseled ends is threaded in along the selvedges for about six inches down each side. A wise choice here is the plain, turned-back hem.

3-5. Black wool tabard, laced at the sides. Laid-in pattern. Weaver, Phyllis Kessel. (Photograph by Kent Kammerer)

Right
3-6. Lace-weave accents neck, armholes, and front of a green wool tabard. Weaver, Phyllis Kessel. (Photograph by Kent Kammerer)

Below
3-7. Detail of lace-weave.

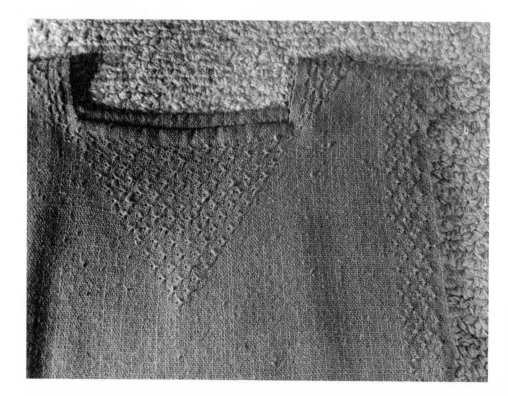

Fine, spring-green wool in two sizes for a more interesting texture is a good background for the subtle lace weave accents in the tabard with lace weave (Figure 3-6). The neck opening is woven in, with the pattern weave in a "V" at the neck and along the arm openings, which are selvedges (Figure 3-7). On each side of the center slit, a band of lace weave is added. Small slits are woven in around the belt line to allow the four-strand braided tie to be threaded through. Warp ends at the bottom are turned back into a narrow, plain hem.

Long Tunic

A long, long, *long* rectangle of double weave forms this tunic (Figure 3–8). The deep, square neck opening is woven in. Black and a dark natural linen are warp, and weft is black. The narrow stripes are woven between bands of loose natural warp. Tapestry-weave shapes here and there provide an interesting pattern. The closures on each side are metal rings, which have been buttonholed with black linen and laced with narrow black grosgrain ribbon whose ends fall to the hemline. The lacing starts high at the underarm and continues to a high waistline, leaving the front and back panels free. The hem is finished with the natural linen in a fringe. This narrow tunic can be worn over a body stocking, slim pants, or skirt and top.

3-8. Long, narrow tunic; one rectangle. Laced high on each side. Double weave. Weaver, Judy Thomas. (Photograph by .Kent Kammerer)

Above
3-9. Black, white, and camel-colored wool. A sleeved tunic. Neckline is faced. By Jan Burhen. (Photograph by Kent Kammerer)

Left
3-10. Muted-plaid wool tunic. Note the off-center neck opening, accenting the lines of the plaid. Leather and button closure. By Jan Burhen. (Photograph by Kent Kammerer)

Opposite
3-11. Diamonds and checks, in purples and gray-green. The V-neck echoes the fabric pattern. A narrow purple leather thong is couched on. By Jan Burhen. (Photograph by Kent Kammerer)

Three-of-a-kind

Unending variety is the fun of these uncomplicated tunics (Figures 3–9, 3–10, and 3–11). Their interest lies in the weave of the fabric and the neck treatment. All are woven, or cut, from a single rectangle with sleeves. All have neck openings large enough to slip over the head easily. They can be worn over a snug body shirt, or as a topper, with or without a scarf to fill in the neckline. These are of soft wool in multiple-harness loom patterns, but would be equally

effective in richly colored plainer weaves, with neck openings woven in. Note how the neck shapes complement the woven patterns. (Also see Figure C–14 and refer to Figure 2–1, typical plan, and the general specifications, page 17.)

The basic RL can be woven in one piece with sleeves as warp extensions, or as additional RLs woven separately. Check the bust and hip measurements closely in planning warp.

Above and opposite
3-12, 3-14. Two views of the Harem Gown. Made of one very wide rectangle, with the fold at the bottom, zippers on the shoulders. By Jan Burhen. (Photograph by Kent Kammerer)

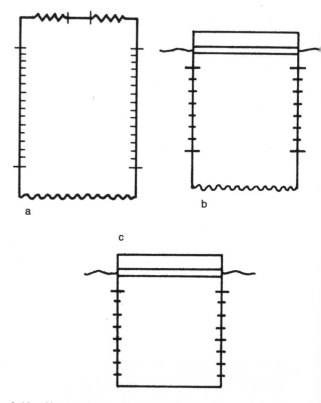

Harem Gown

There are at least three versions of this very long rectangle; two are ankle length with slits for the arms and feet to emerge (Figures 3–13 a, b, c). A short one has a drawstring neckline. They are comfortable, easy to wear and to put together. These are especially fun and colorful when subtle warp color changes are used, not as stripes, but as overall repeats. These give an intriguing glint of color variation, and weave rapidly, as the weft is one color. This rectangle should be made of material that drapes well and is not too bulky so that it will fold gracefully at the bottom.

3-13. Harem Gown. Three versions.

Dimensions

Length: Twice the desired length from neck to floor, knee, or in between.

Width: For the floor-length versions, a yard wide or more in the loom is flowing and comfortable. The short version is best reduced to hip size, plus 4″ finished, plus seaming allowances. If bust measurement is greater, use that, plus. Thus: 36″ hip = 36″ + 4″ + 1½″ + take-up = 42″ total width. Therefore, 21″ in the loom. Remember—you will weave one long RL for front and back.

Directions

Long version (Figure 3–13a). Fold long RL in half, using fold for bottom of dress. If the width is 36″, leave 8″ to 10″ in the center for neck opening. So that the dress will not be too droopy, 8″ is preferred. Insert a zipper on each shoulder seam for ease in putting on. The new invisible zipper makes a finished seam. The zipper and seam allowance are hand-sewn down for the neck facing. The side seam is sewn 8″ from the top and bottom to leave arm and feet openings. The bottom fold becomes a floor crotch. It really isn't awkward!

Note: The side seam on our photographed harem gown is sewn about 6″ in from the selvedges, making an extra drape.

Long version (Figure 3–13b). This is similar to the preceding one in all finishing and folding, but the neck is made by stitching a drawstring tube 1″ down from the top in a 2″ hem. Run in a drawstring of accent color. Draw up to a comfortable fit—it's cool and fluid.

Short version (Figure 3–13c). The RL will need to be cut in half so that the drawstring tube can be formed as described above. The side seams are sewn full length. One or two side slits can be left at the hemline.

To Finish

The individual and decorative touches on this covering should be made in the weaving. The drawstring tube can be woven in, or slits can be woven so that the drawstring can be laced in. An ethnic touch: Tapes or buttons across the top of version *a* relates to the Grecian chiton (Figure 1–4). The top is left entirely open, and buttons and loops join the edges. Buttons may fasten into buttonholes in three or more places, leaving peek-a-boo areas across the arms.

3-16. Black and white tweed, hand-sewn on all edges with black buttonhole stitch. The closures are Danish pewter hooks and eyes. The bottom hem is the attractive selvedge. By Jan Burhen. (Photograph by Kent Kammerer)

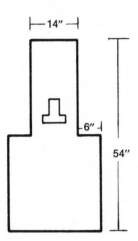

3-15. T-Tunic.

T-Tunic

The plan of this tunic (Figures 3–15, 3–16, 3–17) is a "T" adapted from the long, simple rectangle. The wide section wraps around to meet and fasten in the front. The fastening and neckline are the creative features of this covering.

Dimensions

Length: 54″ (for 5′7″ height). It varies for individual preference.

Width: Widest part of "T" is 26″, narrowing to 14″ for the front. This gives two 6″ side sections for wrap. If you need to vary width to allow for hip measurement, add to these side allowances, leaving center 14″ for medium size. A 12″ center section is adequate for a smaller size (8–10), with proportionate side sections.

To Weave

Begin weaving at the widest end. Weave up 17″. Before beginning narrow weaving for shoulder and front, hemstitch the two 6″ sections while under loom tension. These warp ends can be cut 6″ long and left threaded in the loom if another garment is to be woven on the same warp. The ends will be darned back into the fabric as noted on page 19. You may wish to use separate shut-

tles and weave the 6″ warp sections for use as trim on another tunic. This is time-consuming, but it is worth it to some weavers as a bonus.

Continue weaving for 10″ in the 14″ warp. This is the back armhole allowance.

With two shuttles, begin the neck shaping. For the one in Figure 3–16, a simple, T-shaped neck opening is developed and finished on the loom, using the method described in the loom-shaping section.

Continue weaving the center RL to a length of 54″ total, or the length you require.

To Assemble

No assembling is necessary, as the tunic is all one piece. The wrapped extension can be seamed to the front if you wish. We suggest leaving a 4″ slit at the end of each seam. A zipper could be installed on one side for easy entry. If left open, a variety of closures can be devised—leather, buttons, hooks and eyes, or yarn.

3-17. A view of the tweed tunic, showing the rectangular armhole.

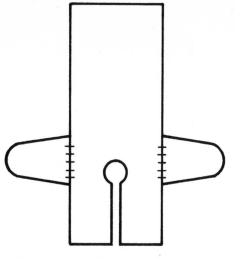

3-18. Portugese Shepherd's Coat.

To Finish

The warp ends at the top of each 6″ section may be knotted for fringe instead of being woven back into the fabric. The hemline may be fringed or hemmed.

Before weaving, consider the closures so that you may create some woven-in details in two or three places at the wrap, to add your own inventive touch.

Portugese Shepherd Coat

Shepherds in Portugal wear a warm garment that is part coat, part cape. It seems to be a very practical style for the work they do, as is true of coverings that evolve from materials at hand, worn effectively. A refinement of the practice of throwing a cured sheepskin over the shoulders, this coat retains the shaping of the skin. Worn with the fleece side out as in our illustration (Figure C–8), the shoulder and upper arm extension has been rounded and shaped. All around the edge, the fleece has been cut off to the skin, making a flat band. From the front, the top looks like a waist-length jacket. The shoulders widen into oval, cape-like sections which cover the upper arm. The back reaches well below the knees. So, this shepherd, working with his flock in cold or wet weather, is protected on back and shoulders with a comforting layer of coat. His arms are partly covered, but free of a confining sleeve. No long, cumbersome front will get in the way while he is walking or running after his charges. A truly functional, indigenous—and handsome—garment.

We picture this as a rather high-style modern coat, woven of richly hand-spun wool, with decorative woven, or embroidered, bands for trim and waistband across the front.

Dimensions

Proportions are dictated by the wearer, with length from back hem to shoulder, and shoulder front to waistline added to get the total length. The width will be sufficient to cover the back at least to where the side seam would fall. If you weave the extended shoulder sections as part of the body section, your warp will be the width necessary for that.

To Weave

Weave your wool in one long rectangle, extending the arm cover as woven, or weave extra shaped sections to be added to a long, straight body section as in Figure 3–18. Start weaving at the bottom back hem. First weave a patterned band. Then continue until you reach the neck. With two shuttles, weave a slightly shaped neckline. Continue weaving the two front sections. The same patterned band can be woven at the end of each side. The same band can also be woven at one, or both, ends of separate sleeve sections. To relate even more to the original, a low pile weave might be woven on all, or part, of the fabric. Pile-weave bands would be effective instead of patterned ones. We think this coat plan has many exciting possibilities.

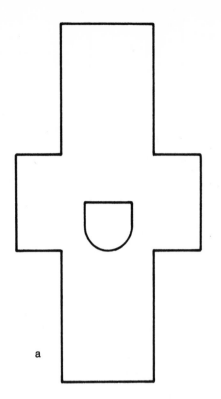

a

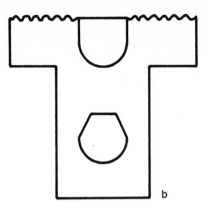

3-19. African Shirt.

b

African Shirt

This garment (Figure 3–19 a, b) is an adaptation of an African shirt, with a surprise use of the cut-out-neck section. Wear it as a shirt or a topper over pants, or a long or short skirt. Make it long enough for a dress, or wear it over a body shirt. Weave it in one long rectangle with sleeves woven and added, or weave it on a warp wide enough to allow the sleeve extensions to be fashioned as part of the body. This shirt also can easily be cut from woven yardage. The really delightful part of this design is what happens to the shape cut out for the neck opening. It becomes the pocket! A very ornamental detail can be done here, with the pocket applied with decorative stitches. It can be completely embroidered before sewing on; appliquéd; beaded, or otherwise decorated.

Dimensions

The measurements are your own—depending upon the length you want, the amount of sleeve, and the size of neck opening/pocket.
Length: 60″ total finished. Allow extra for hem or fringe.
Width: Widest in loom is 45″ for sleeves woven onto the garment.

To Weave

Two ways of weaving are suggested:

On a wide loom, 45″ in the loom, or on a 24″ loom, weave a RL, and weave the sleeves separately.

To weave the wide, whole garment on a 36″ to 45″ loom; weave the back 22″ wide, for 20″ where the sleeve extensions will be woven for the full width.

Note: The 11½″ of warp on each side of the weaving may be left threaded in front of the heddles. This will be picked up and threaded through the reed when 20″ has been reached and you are ready to weave in the sleeves. These thrums are useful for the pocket embroidery, and are by no means wasted!

To weave on a 24″ loom, with sleeves woven separately:
Length: 60″ finished length, as above.
Width: 22″ wide woven for the length needed.

Two ways for sleeves to be woven:
Weave 12″ for each sleeve. This will be folded

in half lengthwise and joined to the center RL when assembling.

For wrist-length sleeves, weave 21″ long; fold in half weftwise.

The Neck-opening/Pocket

The neck is cut out and used as a pocket appliqué at the center front. Figure 3–19a shows a suggested shape, but the scope is unlimited for shapes, sizes, and placement.

Consider a deep oval neckline. The bottom of the pocket is rounded. The upper corners may be folded down for ease of inserting the hands (Figure 3–19b). Sew to the shirt at center top of the pocket, and around the lower part up to the folded down corners. A large rectangle cut out of the neck opening will give you a wide pocket to apply at the center or the side.

To Assemble

The shirt is flat-joined on the sides, leaving a 4″ slit from the bottom. It is wise to double-stitch around the neck opening before cutting it out.

Place pocket and sew to the shirt as suggested.

To Finish

The neck may be bound with a buttonhole stitch, or faced with a lining material. The pocket is the key feature, and should be fastened in place with a special stitch.

Another Method

The pocket may also be shaped separately, or woven or cut from the cloth. The neck opening can be shaped on the loom as detailed in other shirts. One important consideration is to keep the opening small enough to fit and allow the head through, but still not make it too large. If you want a really big cut-out pocket, the neckline can be a deep one, and the topper worn over a body shirt, jumper-style. But we like the whole concept of this design—using the cut-out as an applied pocket. This is what gives the shirt its individuality.

A different style of shirt, from West Africa, is pictured in Figure 1–11, and the method of adding triangles is detailed on page 48.

3-21. Slip-over poncho with knitted turtleneck is one yard square. Weaver, Harriette Gardner; knitter, Noel Hammock. (Photograph by Kent Kammerer)

3-20.

ONE SQUARE

A 36″ square becomes a slipover poncho. Weave a square, adding a few contrasting "racing stripes." Then cut out an oval hole for the neck. Figure 3–21 shows one with a 7″ x 9″ opening. Triple-stitch on the machine around the cut edge and sew on a bias binding. Knit and purl a turtleneck, adding stripes to match those on the cloth. Decrease a few rows and then increase so that the collar will taper slightly in and out for better fit. Twirl the poncho around your neck to wear it any way that pleases you—with points in front and back, straight across, the stripes up and down, or horizontal. This one is made from worsted synthetic yarn, and can be tossed into the washer-dryer. Try color combinations such as navy with stripes of light blue, green, and white; dark green with orange, white, and blue; or brown with orange, yellow, and white.

3-22.

ONE RECTANGLE, LONG, NARROW, WITH ADDITIONS

Infinite variety is possible when you add squares, triangles, or more rectangles to the basic single rectangle of the body of a garment. Our examples, following, are just a point of departure, and we know that you will have many more ideas. Small units are added for better fit, to enlarge narrow weaving, or to create a more sophisticated body covering.

Lengthy Tunic

This tunic is best made floor length as a simple rectangle with sleeves added. The yardage should be of simple elegance, featuring decorative seam joinings (see Figure 3–23 a, b, c, d).

Dimensions

Length: Shoulder-to-ankle length (or shorter, if preferred) x 2 for front and back, plus the 3″ hem on each end of the RL. Warp length will include sleeve length, as described below.

Width: for a medium size, weave 22″, which includes the side-seam allowance. Remember: check your hip and bust measurements.

Sleeves: The sleeve length and width are your own preference. We suggest an 18″ length and a 20″ finished width around for each sleeve, folded warpwise.

For narrower sleeves: Weave less than 18″ and fold widthwise. Length can be adjusted when assembled.

To Weave

The body RL: On a 22″-wide warp, weave your length to the shoulder. Shape the neck as chosen. A simple horizontal 2″-wide slit complements the simplicity and lends itself to decorative stitchery.

Weave your choice of sleeve size, as above.

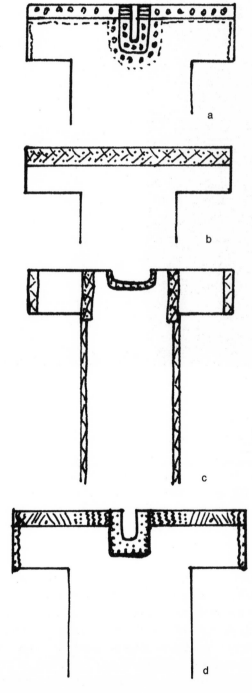

3-23. Lengthy tunic.

To Assemble

First add sleeves to the center RL; then sew sleeve and side seams. Sleeves are sewn into the RL with a flat seam if selvedges are joined. A flat felled seam may be stitched. If the sleeve is too long, cut the shoulder end of the sleeve, or turn back in a cuff at the wrist.

To Finish

Put in the hem. If a fine warp is used, a short fringe is attractive here. Put decorative stitching on the neck and sleeve seams. Let your creative fingers run free, and use several embroidery stitches in rows in several colors. Or embroider rich bands of stitches in one matching, or contrasting yarn. Note the Coptic placement of bands and roundels (Figure 1–1, a b, c).

Laurie Coat

A variation of the sleeved tunic, this coat is woven with an open front (Figures 3–24, 3–25). We call it a "Laurie Coat" because it was highly developed by Laurie Herrick of Arts and Crafts, Portland, Oregon. We have seen many variations, some with block areas of color and subtle patterns in color. Ours is of curly mohair and very fine smooth wool, in green-gold and gold. It is a simple version, plain weave. This style is a perfect background for embellishment, and one day we plan to do some stitchery along the front opening. For now, we vary the look with different pins as closures, or let it remain open and unadorned. This is full length, with warp fringe at sleeves and bottom hem. It can be any length you wish, from short jacket to ankle length. The neckline is shaped on the loom, with warp ends darned in later. Seams are invisible, especially in a textured yarn such as mohair. It is woven as one rectangle, full width for the back. Then the neckline is shaped and the weaving continued with two shuttles. The two fronts are woven at the same time. Extra lengths are woven for the sleeves, which are cut and sewn to the body of the coat.

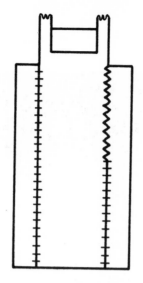

3-26.   Sleeveless jumper.

Sleeveless Jumper

Add two narrow rectangles to the long basic rectangle with neck slit, and you have a sleeveless jumper (Figure 3–26). It can be worn with or without a blouse. This slipover is easily woven and assembled. Make it any length—from tunic, to jumper, to ankle length. You will find it useful and easy to wear. The simple joining is a fine place for stitches to accent the seams.

Dimensions

Length: Any length you desire, from shoulder down, x 2 for front and back, plus hems or fringe. Width: Our standard 14″ for medium size is best used in this garment. The side additions will be one-half that width. Remember this is a *finished* width; thus, seam allowances must be added for woven width.

Note: Bust and hip measurements are critical in measuring the width for this pattern. If bust is much less than hip, it would be desirable to taper the side additions, making them narrower at the top.

To Weave

Weave the center RL, with shaped neck of any design, to the length required.

Weave two side panels 7″, *finished* width, with two shuttles.

To Assemble

Side panels are joined to body RL 8″ down from shoulder fold, which forms the arm opening. For easiest entry, put an 18″ zipper (Unique—invisible) in the left front seam.

To Finish

The seams and neckline are two areas that can be enhanced by special treatment, such as rows of stitchery. Perhaps you will devise another closure in the left seam instead of the zipper.

Jump Suit or Pants-dress

One elongated rectangle with slit-weave ends, plus added rectangles for sleeves and easement equals a one-piece jump suit (Figure 3–27 a, b). It can be left sleeveless for the addition of a sweater or shirt.

Dimensions

Weave a length from ankle up over the shoulders and down to ankle, plus enough for sleeves. Also weave a 12″-wide RL to fit on the inside of the leg and crotch. The length is determined by the length of the slits for the legs. This allows for ease of movement and eliminates puckering in the front and back of the center RL. Measure the width, allowing enough for easy fit when the leg sections are sewn. This should be a generous fit, and the excess can be gathered into a belt or sash.

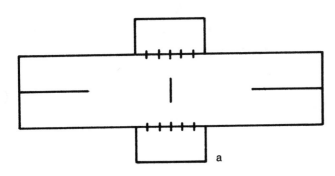

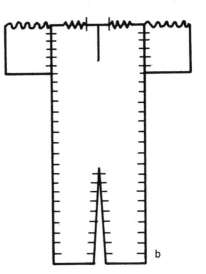

3-27. Jumpsuit or pants dress.

Note: In your planning, decide on a method of entry. This garment was made up the first time, only to find there was no way to get into it! Some suggested ways to allow for large enough opening are:

Weave a vertical slit up the back to neckline for a zipper or other closure.

Extend the neck opening at the shoulder fold, making a slit which can be closed in either decorative or inconspicuous fashion.

To Weave
Begin weaving with two shuttles, leaving a slit long enough to reach from ankle to crotch. Then continue weaving the full width, with one shuttle, until you reach the neck. A shaped neckline, or slit, can be woven here. (See note above on providing entry.) Then continue the full width, weaving to where the back slit starts for the crotch to ankle. Leave space for fringe at the bottom of the legs. Weave enough for a small hem, or weave the exact length and bind. Weave enough for the sleeves—the length from shoulder to elbow or wrist—leaving space for fringe, or add length for seam and hem. Fringe can be at the shoulder joining and/or at the bottom of the sleeve. Weave the section for crotch easement, providing the same hem treatment as that on the legs.

To Assemble
After removing from the loom, cut off the two sleeve pieces (first stitching the cut edges). Fold the body length, and join the side seams. Add the easement RLs to each leg seam. Join the leg seams. Finish the hems of legs and sleeves.

To Finish
Add hand stitches to any of the seams, feature the closures, or add a pocket or two.

A Variation
This design can be made on a small loom, weaving two narrow RLs in place of the one wide RL. The design, dimensions, shape, and assembling are essentially the same. The center RLs will be joined front and back in the body of the garment. A zipper could be inserted in front or back seam. If you want to feel unbound in a suit like this, a gusset may be put in the crotch for easement.

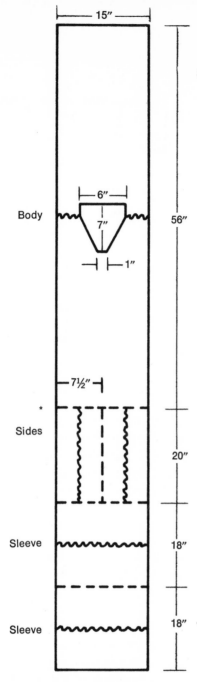

15″

a

3-28. Sleeved tunic.

Body

6″

7″

1″

56″

7½″

*

Sides

20″

Sleeve

18″

Sleeve

18″

*Leave space for fringe here.

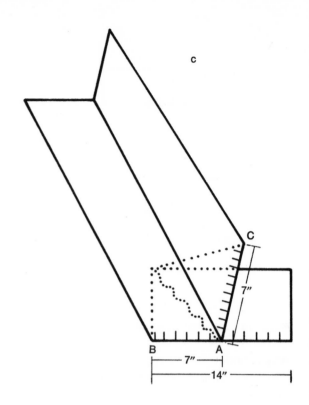

c

C

7″

B   A

7″

14″

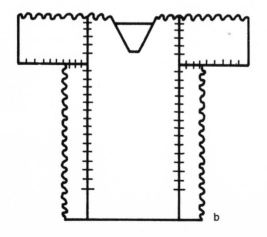

b

Sleeved Tunic

This tunic is easy and comfortable to wear and easy to make (Figures 3–28 a, b, c, 3–29, 3–30). It is based on a series of 14″ finished width rectangles. Any desired length is satisfactory. Our example is 28″.

Dimensions

Length: Measure the front and back lengths. Refer to the description of Figure 3–28a for the measurements we used.

Width: Weave on a warp to produce 14″ width. Allow for weaving take-up according to your yarn and your own beat. When the selvedges are flat-needle-joined, 14″ is adequate. Allow 1½″ extra when a stitched seam is necessary.

Neck opening: The woven neck opening is wedge-shaped, tapering from 6″ at the shoulder, to 1″ at the base. From shoulder to bottom, the neck opening is 7″ deep.

Sleeves: Two woven rectangles, 18″ long, are folded for a finished sleeve, 16″ around.

Side sections: Weave 20″ long. Finished width in garment is 7½″.

3-29. Sleeved tunic. Soft wool, in shades of gray-green. Vents at each seam, front and back. A deep facing is added across the shoulders. Weaver, Jan Burhen. (Photograph by Kent Kammerer)

To Weave

At beginning and end of the body RL, leave warp space, or weave extra for the hem finish you plan. Weave the body RL to 27″ before beginning the neck shaping. Using two shuttles, form the neck opening, gradually widening it from 1″ to 6″. Continue for 7″ up to the shoulder. It is well to make a pattern, or template, to guide you in this shaping. Refer to the loom-shaping section for more complete directions on this procedure. Continue weaving 28″ for the back.

A second RL is woven for the side sections. This may be woven full width and cut down the center for two panels, or two shuttles may be used to weave the two strips simultaneously, each having two selvedges. The length is 20″, plus fringe or hem allowance. Completed width for each panel will be about 7½″. For sleeves, weave two 18″ RLs. These will be folded in half and seamed.

To Assemble

These directions may seem lengthy, but each step is easy, and following the procedures step-by-step will simplify it further.

Joining method: Selvedges are joined together with an invisible flat-join, with needle and matching yarn. When all pieces are woven as suggested, this is a neat, simple finish. If the edges are less than perfect, or if you are cutting some of the pieces from yardage, it would be wise to follow the directions on seaming process, below. Figure 3–29 is seamed from a piece of handwoven yardage. Whether seaming or flat-joining, the order of assembling is the same.

Seaming process: For cut edges, first edge with seam tape, stitching by machine. This will give a smoother, custom finish. The binding should be lightly whipped down by hand to complete the seam. If edges are selvedge, there is no need to bind with tape, but they should be whipped down by hand.

To put it all together: Neck and lower edges should be completed before assembling. Refer to Figure 3–28c for detail.

Fold the center RL in half, with the right side out.

Fold the 18″ sleeve rectangle in half, with selvedges at right and left, wrong side out. Seam allowance is 2″ (plus seam binding, if used). Stitch seam from the end of the sleeve toward the joining end. Stitch only to 7″ from the joining end. Lock the stitches and remove from the machine.

Fold the side additions in half, lengthwise, wrong side out. The top of the addition will now be seamed together with the sleeve. Put wrong sides together and pin the center fold on the side addition into the sleeve seam opening. The 14″ dimension of each section should match.

Insert needle at sleeve terminal 7″ in from edge, stitching end A. Stitch side and sleeve together to B. Repeat on seam A–C. Be sure that no hole appears at apex A in stitching. This can be reinforced with a second stitching.

Turn inside out to form sleeve and side, as shown. Repeat for opposite side.

Note: This is the same assembling method used in the "Burhenoose," page 81, before attaching hood section.

Attaching the sleeve section to the body RL is simply one continuous seam, matching the top of the sleeve with the top of center RL.

An easier fit is achieved by leaving the seams open for 3″ or 4″ at the bottom, front, and/or back, as desired.

Figure 3–29, of handwoven wool, has a neck facing of fine lining material. This is a good idea, especially in a loosely woven fabric. Extend the facing to the edge of center RL and join in the seam to anchor.

3-30. Three tunics of patterned or textured wool. All by Jan Burhen. (Photograph by Kent Kammerer)

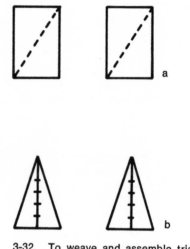

3-32. To weave and assemble triangles.

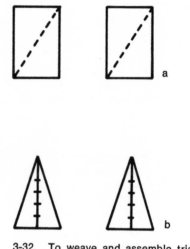 3-31. Triangles.

ADDING TRIANGLES TO THE BASIC RECTANGLE

Triangles—from squares or rectangles, or woven to a triangular shape—are added to a rectangle for flare, easement, an A-line, or sleeves (Figure 3–33).

Adding Triangles as Side Inserts

Weave the basic long RL for back and front. Put in a neck opening while weaving, or cut one in later. Weave an additional amount—2 x the length needed for the insert in one side. This will be cut on the diagonal to form two triangles (Figure 3–32a). These, in turn, may be joined to form an equilateral triangle for one side (Figure 3–32b). A more elaborate weaving procedure to obtain two triangles for side additions with no seam in the center, and with selvedges all around, is to weave them on a board-and-nail loom with warp in the shape and size triangle needed. See Figure 3–34 for the African child's loom—one more version of weaving a triangle.

Another way is to weave in tapestry technique on the warp used for the RL sections. The warp ends could be incorporated into an interesting fringe where the triangles are joined to the sides—a different, integral design.

Right
3-33.   Detail of a triangular addition, set into the side of a silk kimono. All hand-sewn, completely lined. (Photograph by Beverly Rush)

Below
3-34.   Ashanti boys learn to weave on a small triangular loom. Sketch shows how the woven pieces are sewn together. Bonwire, Ghana. From *Introducing West African Cloth*, by Kate P. Kent, with permission of the author and the Denver Museum of Natural History.

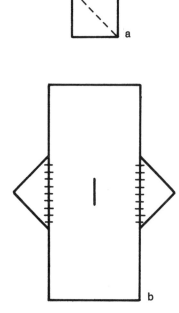

3-35.   Triangles added as sleeves.

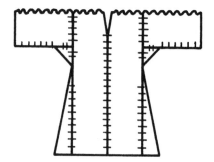

3-36.   Triangular flares.

Triangles Added as Sleeves

A covering for the upper arm, woven as shown, is a graceful addition to the simple sheath. Cut a square of fabric on the diagonal (see Figures 3–35a, b). Sew to the RL of the body with the cut edge along the selvedge. Place it to fall over the shoulder and upper arm. The raw edge can be put under the selvedge edge and fancy stitches, woven bands, fringe, or other embellishment applied to accent the line. If you prefer, the two sleeve triangles can be woven to shape as described above, and you will have selvedges to work with.

Triangular Flares

A one-rectangle dress with flares is shown in Figure 3–36. Two rectangles are added for sleeves. Two rectangles are cut, sewn into triangles, and then inserted for side flares.

Dimensions

The important measurements to consider are the bust, hip, and length. These will determine your center RL warp dimensions.

To Weave

The triangle-insert RLs are best woven the length necessary. Use one-half of the warp width for each, and weave both RL inserts simultaneously, with two shuttles. This keeps all pattern, or warp, in the garment going in the same direction.

The sleeve RLs may be woven either vertically, or horizontally, on the loom. The neckline opening, or slit, can be cut in later, or woven in.

To Assemble

Match selvedges and seam the triangles and sleeves to the side seams. Fold and seam the sleeves.

To Finish

If you like, emphasize any or all seams with top handstitching. An elaborate embroidered neckline, or embroidered yoke to the sleeve seam, would be appropriate on this graceful dress.

Triangles Added in a Shirt

A man's shirt from Africa is made of narrow striped strips in the shape of a slipover rectangular tunic. Narrow triangles are set in, starting about at the waistline. The triangles are cut from plain white strips, diagonally, and the straight selvedge sides are stitched on the wrong side in a conventional seam. The slanting, cut side is stitched, on the top, to the next striped section in a top-stitched seam. This gives a slight flare to the bottom of the shirt. One quite detailed shirt had an additional straight piece set into each side, with a pocket worked into it. Ornamental borders of machine stitching in several colors were worked around the pocket opening, much like the ornamental rows of stitching around necklines on African shirts.

This idea could be adapted for use in a skirt —long or short. It is a decorative and subtle way to add a gentle tapering to a rectangular garment. The man's tunic in Figure 1–11 is from northern Ghana, and is similar to this.

Weaving Triangles the Ashanti Way
Ashanti boys learn weaving on a simple loom fastened to a plank (Figure 3–34). The warp is triangular in shape, and the resulting triangles of cloth are sewn together to make long rectangular strips like their Kente cloth. This is one more idea for weaving shapes to add, with selvedges all around.

Variations on the Theme
The basic 14″-wide woven rectangles suggest a number of variations and ways to weave and use these shapes.

Weave an extra length, fold it in half, and put it around the middle. If your yarns are bulky, either weave this length in a finer yarn—matching, contrast, patterned—or weave a narrower RL and use the single layer. This serves to hold the front and back in place when you do not join the side seams, and it makes a sleeveless short jumper top. The warp ends can be braided or knotted for a closing.

This added piece can be sewn on as part of the topper, or used as a belt or sash. This idea seems to stem from the Japanese obi, which is wide, doubled, and used to hold the wrapped-over kimono in place.

Refer to Figures 5–3 and 5–4 for Judy Thomas's pocket belts. These would be perfect to use in the manner just described.

On a plain tunic—sleeved or not—apply narrow woven bands or belts. Use several. They will serve as closures as well as decoration. They can be sewn or buttoned, just at the sides, or used to encircle the garment.

Experiment with these ideas. You will find other ways to fasten, secure, or otherwise add to your plain basic tunics and shirts.

3-37.

ONE RECTANGLE, WIDE

Simple Jacket
This jacket is a refinement of a wide rectangle wrapped about like a blanket (Figures 3–38, 3–39, 3–40). It can be constructed on the loom, except for the shoulder seams, or it can be made from yardage already woven. In this case, the arm slits must be cut and finished. It can be woven two ways, depending upon the size of the loom.

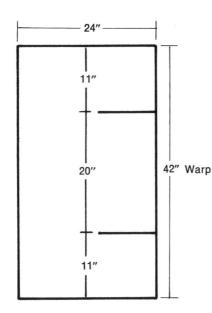

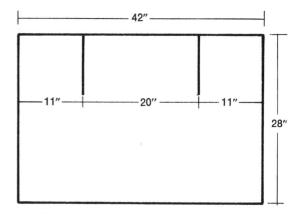

3-39. Simple jacket, woven on wide loom.

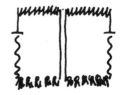

3-40. Simple jacket, finishing ideas.

3-38. Simple jacket, woven on narrow loom.

Dimensions

The length and width will vary according to need and preference. The proportions should be planned for comfortable wearability. Arm slits: Slits are left open to the top of the shoulder for ease of wear and appearance. The slit should be a minimum of 10″. For a man, or for an easier fit, 15″ would be best.

The jacket can be woven horizontally on a 45″, or wider, loom (Figure 3–39). The warp ends will be at top and bottom, and the arm slits will be done in slit-weave (kelim tapestry technique). Note that this version is woven longer as a pre-ference—an advantage if weaving it widthwise.

To Assemble

Join the top edges from arm slits to desired neck opening. This can be done with flat-seamed join-ing, or with a decorative finish stitch.

To Finish

Because this is such a simple jacket, you have much leeway in the hem, shoulder, and closing details (Figure 3–40). Just a few of the many ways are suggested here—work out your favorites.

Wide-woven: Warp ends are tied together, joining at the shoulders with a fringe trim. Warp ends at the bottom are knotted or plaited. Note the carefully plaited fringe on the poncho, Figure 4–13.

Narrow-woven: Warp ends are along the front opening edges and can be left as fringe, turned back in a hem, or darned in. Some longer warp ends can be left for braiding into ties for casual closures.

3-41. "Kiskimil."

Kiskimil

Our "Kiskimil," Figure 3–41 is presented with apologies to the Mexican quechquemitl for our version of its name. This variation of the two-rectangle shawl is worn in some areas of Mexico. Very small versions of it are even worn as head coverings. The design is the same, simply scaled down to fit the head, with points in front and back.

Dimensions

As it can be woven in either direction, the yardage will be determined by loom width. It is most simply woven on a wide loom and, since it takes so little yardage—about 24″ plus fringe—a number of them with great variety could be woven on one multi-colored warp. If fringe is desired, plan approximately one yard per shawl.

To Weave

This wide RL is folded in half to form a square. As it is woven, a slit is formed on the fold line with two shuttles.

Wide Loom: Weave a RL 45″ wide by 22½″ long, plus fringe allowance. Weave an 8″ slit as indicated in Figure 3–41, with two shuttles, in kelim tapestry technique. Provision for fringe may be left top and bottom. See finishing details that follow.

Narrow Loom: Weave a RL 24″ or 30″ wide, remembering to double the length for a square

when folded in half. When 24″ are woven, form the slit by throwing the shuttle from left for 16″ and back to left selvedge. Continue weaving in this fashion for a few inches. Finish the top and bottom edge of the slit with a buttonhole stitch while in tension. Complete the weaving of the RL. Leave ample length for plain, or knotted, fringe on warp at both ends of RL.

To Assemble

Fold the RL in half on the slit line. Join the top of the RL as indicated in Figure 3–41, leaving 8″ for the neck opening. Joining may be made with needle stitches, or you may tie warp ends together. If the RL is woven widthwise, this makes an interesting off-balance design.

To Finish

Fringe may be knotted along the lower edge. It may also be added onto the selvedges for continuous fringes. If fringe is not desired, turn the warp ends into a narrow hem.

The 8″ corner—front and back—is folded down for the neck opening. This may be made unimportant by folding it inside, catching it lightly by hand sewing, or it can be made an important feature with creative decoration on the outside. Study the beautiful embroideries and woven patterns in Mexican and Guatemalan textiles for patterns and color.

3-42. Primitive wrap—just one wide rectangle. Bands of pattern are woven in contrasting color.

3-43. The closure. Simple, appropriate, and easy to use. Woven by Jan Burhen. (Photographs by Kent Kammerer)

Primitive Wrap

With an imaginative use of a loom-threaded pattern, you can weave a handsome coat as one wide rectangle. As it is wide enough to provide a drop shoulder, it can be worn with short sleeves, but is most useful and looks best when worn over a long-sleeved top.

The neckline is shaped while weaving. The front laps over several inches. Jan Burhen's coat is woven of nubby black wool and homespun burnt-orange wool. Threaded to a diamond twill, the bands of contrasting pattern are slimming and give that special handwoven look. Edges of the sleeves, sides, and fronts are selvedges. The selvedges are overlapped at the sides to give a slight shaping before release to make the armhole. The neckline is finished with hand stitching to bind. Note the closure—a horn button with cord of matching wool sewn on the opposite side, which is then wrapped around the button to secure it.

3-44. The Kbee Koat is so wearable, so weavable, we show it in two fabrics. This one is woven on the same colorful warp as the Burhenoose (Figures 3-86, 3-87, and front cover), but with a finer wool weft.

3-45. Detail to show the hand-sewn joining across the yoke and sleeves. Note the careful matching of stripes. Weaver, Jan Burhen. (Photographs by Kent Kammerer)

Kbee Koat

The Kbee Koat is an original design developed by Jan Burhen and Helen Kerr ("Kbee" is a combination of the initials of the two designer-weavers). Intrigued with what the loom would allow, and with a growing interest in primitive style garments, Jan experimented with paper-folding and came up with the pattern and weaving directions for this handsome, wearable, and undated coat (see Figures 3–44 through 3–48). Truly a loom-fashioned garment, with just two cuts, it allows great leeway for color, stripes, and

3-46. Bronze-brown homespun with line stripes in gold-green. This shows clearly the over-all shape of the Kbee Koat, the yoke join, and placement of the striping.

3-47, 3-48. Details of sleeve, yoke, and closure, on and off the figure. Woven by Jan Burhen. (Photographs by Kent Kammerer)

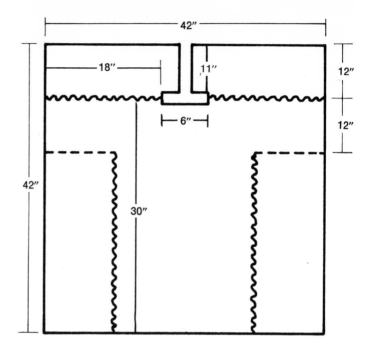

3-49. Kbee Koat, plan.

joining details. It can be any length you wish—from fingertip to ankle; it can be lightweight or heavy. As testimony to its classic, dateless look and changeability, we show one of subtle shading (Figure 3–46) and one that reflects splashy, primitive coloring (Figure 3–44 and C–17).

Dimensions
One wide rectangle is woven as a single unit, with the neck opening fashioned on the loom in the last 12″ of the RL. (See Figure 3–49.)
Length: Measure the length from shoulder to the desired length when finished (30″ preferred). Add 12″ for the front and sleeve. The total is 42″ for the entire coat.
Width: Hip measurement, plus 6″ for ease and loom take-up. Our examples are 45″ and 48″ in the loom.
Neck opening: 6″ wide by 2″ deep.
Front opening: 11″ from neck.

To Weave
If you are using warp stripes, plan the stripe reversal very carefully. Study the pattern diagram to find just where the stripes will occur. This is a nice design challenge. Try to come up with an interesting arrangement of colors, spacing, and pattern. Note the two entirely different stripe placements in our two examples.

Refer to Figure 3–49. Weave 30″. Then, using two shuttles, begin to fashion a 6″ neck opening. Measure from the center and weave an 18″-wide section on each side of the warp for two inches, which leaves a neck opening 6″ wide and 2″ deep. See note below for finishing this opening. Continue weaving with two shuttles from each side to the center and return, leaving a slit 11″ long at the center front. This section is your neck and sleeve.

Note: It is preferable to finish the neckline on the loom while the warp is in tension. Work a buttonhole stitch around the opening between the warp threads. When taken from the loom, these warp ends can be cut and darned into the back and two front sides of the opening.

To Assemble
Study the dotted lines on the cutting diagram and the directions *very* carefully, as the cut is made to separate the sleeve and body of the coat (Figures 3–49 and 3–50).

Lay the RL out flat.

Fold 12″ down from the neck opening to form sleeves.

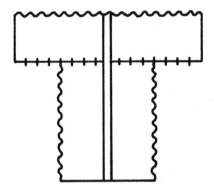

3-50. Kbee Koat.

Measure the width of the RL and divide this number by four. This is the number of inches you will cut in from the edge just below the sleeve allowance. A precaution! Stitch on each side of the cutting line *before* cutting to keep the edges from raveling. This is especially important in a heavy, handwoven textile. Then fold the cut sides to the center of the garment. Selvedges should line up with the neck edges, forming sleeves. As in our illustration, sleeves will be 10½″ in length from the body of the coat. The sleeve is seamed together with an overlap of ⅜″. Seam the yoke in the same way. This is best done on a machine for strength and then covered with a decorative stitch.

To Finish
The closure is the only finishing touch necessary. It can be a piece of suitable jewelry—fun to vary and change. A decorative hook and eye, frog, or tie may be used. Refer to our suggested closures, pages 115-18, and be sure to choose one that is appropriate and of the right material to complement your fabric.

3-51.

TWO RECTANGLES, LONG AND NARROW

The least complicated method of using two long, narrow rectangles is, simply, to sew the two strips together for the full length, leaving the seam open for the head. Call it a serape or a poncho. (See Figures 3–52 and 3–53.)

Dimensions
Size for whatever length or width you desire. It can be worn with the neck slit at the center back and front, or from shoulder to shoulder. The joining seam can be an important detail of design, or inconspicuous.

To Weave
Two x the length, in the width you decide is right.

To Assemble
Cut your long RL into two shorter RLs and join, leaving a neck slit.

To Finish
The cut hems can be fringed, hemmed, bound, or otherwise finished.

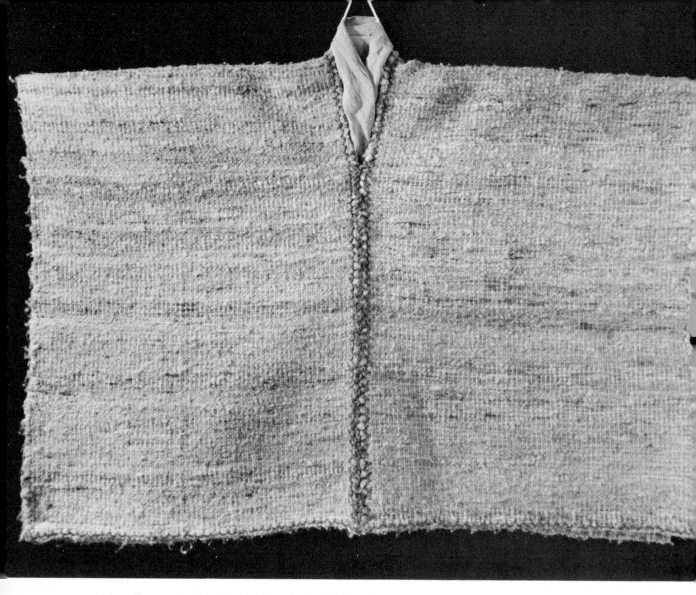

3-52. Two rectangles joined with raised chain band stitch. Of unspun gray and gray-green nettle-dyed wool. Woven by author.

3-53. Nettle poncho, showing the draping. (Photographs by Kent Kammerer)

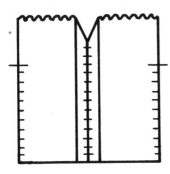

3-54. Sleeveless jacket.

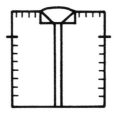

3-55. Janus jacket.

Nettle-dyed Poncho

This poncho is woven of unspun natural gray and white wool that has been dyed a soft grayed green with nettle broth. Its dimensions let it become a cozy cover when you are sitting. The joining stitches are raised chain band and Y-stitch. The Y-stitch continues on around the neck opening and is worked at the hemline also to help secure the hem and unify the design (Figures 3–52 and 3–53).

Sleeveless Jacket

This jacket (Figure 3–54) is a version of the poncho above—two strips joined—but it is joined only up the back to the neck. The front is left open. It is put on over the shoulders and does not have to slip on over the head. Fasteners such as cord frogs, a metal hooked clasp, crossover lacings, or other means will serve to hold it in place and add a nice touch. A woven, leather, or macramé belt can be worn over the front and around under the back. The sleeveless jacket is also a relative of the South American *ruana*. A real ruana is open up the front and has a collar. Sometimes the four corners are rounded. The sides are left open and unsewn, fastened only with a button inside. See Figure 4–13 in the loom-shaped section for a poncho styled like those from Ecuador.

Janus Jacket

A two-faced fabric—natural gray and white unspun wool and fine beige raw silk on the outside and off-white raw silk on the inside is used for this jacket (Figures 3–55, 3–56, and 3–57). The weave is four harness, 3/1 twill. We have classified this, in turn, as a single rectangle, then as cut and sewn. But we have placed it here because it is similar to the sleeveless jacket. We chose this cut shoulder style for the heavy, unyielding fabric so that the seam could be tapered for a better fit.

Dimensions

Measure the width needed across the shoulders and hips in back. The length will be twice the length from shoulder to hem. This one is about fingertip length.

To Weave

Weave one long RL twice the length of shoulder to hemline. The turn of the unspun weft at the selvedges was purposely made loose to give a small puff.

To Assemble and Finish

Cut the long RL in two, widthwise. Stitch, or secure, the cut edges to keep from raveling. Then cut one piece in half lengthwise for the two fronts. Place the selvedge of the back section on top of the cut edge of the front, and sew by hand with matching yarn. We used raw silk. The cut edge inside was later sewn over by hand with

Above

3-56. Janus Jacket. Double-faced, 3/1 twill. Gray and white unspun wool outside, raw silk inside.

Right

3-57. Detail, sleeve and neck edges. Note ancient Mexican clay spindle whorls for closure. Woven by author. (Photographs by Kent Kammerer)

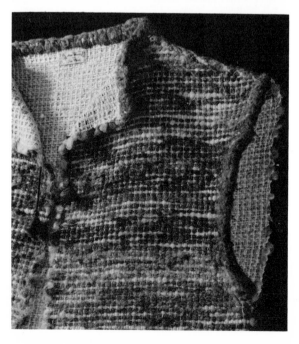

the silk in a buttonhole stitch. The selvedges are the front edges. At the back of the neck, we cut a shallow ellipse for more comfortable fit. The cut edges of the neck line were covered with a heavy buttonhole stitch of the gray unspun wool. Shoulder seams, slightly tapered, were sewn by hand. The seam was not trimmed—just folded back, flattened with pressing, and lightly sewn down. The corners at the chin turn back to show the white silk "lining." Small, ancient carved clay spindle whorls from Mexico, threaded and knotted onto narrow thongs, are the closing (Figure 3–57).

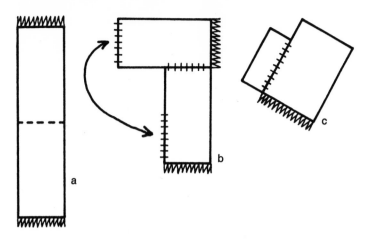

3-58. Quechquemitl.

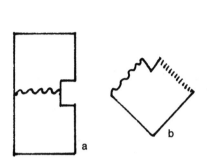

3-59. An unusual quechquemitl.

Quechquemitl

The quechquemitl—a Mexican shoulder covering—is easy to put on and as useful as a sweater (Figures 3–58 to 3–66, and C–12). A study of these shawls becomes surprisingly complex. There is great variation in ways of wearing, methods of construction, designs, sizes, and customs. It is a fascinating subject, and we suggest it for further study. Mexican ones are cotton, silk, or wool; embroidered, gauze weave, brocade weave, stripes, tie-dyed, or knotted. Sometimes they are combinations of these. While they are usually worn as a shoulder covering, a Huichol way is to wear handwoven ones as a head covering (Figure C–1). The neck opening is put on to fit snugly across the forehead. The cloth is turned back to cover the top of the head and hang down. Quite a familiar covering, popular with weavers, they appear in many versions, all kinds of material and a number of techniques—woven, knitted, crocheted, macramé. The pattern works very well when cut from handwoven, or other, yardage. Weave it on any loom—threaded pattern, plain weave, twill, or whatever suits your yarn and design. Colors are unlimited. Fringes can be plain or fancy. Add wool tassels as the Mexicans sometimes do. See the one woven of fur strips (Figures 3–64, 3–65, 3–66, and C–12). They are made from just one basic rectangle, cut in half and reassembled at right angles. Any of them are worn with points front and back, or straight across.

Dimensions

Length: Your choice is for your need. It can be variable. A good length to weave is 86″. Cut it into two lengths of 43″ each.
Width: Also variable. A comfortable width is 17″ to 19″. A finished piece of fabric about 65″ x 28″, plus fringe, is adequate.

To Weave

Allow several inches for fringe at the beginning of the weaving, and again at the end. If you plan to do some elaborate knotting, allow plenty of extra warp length. Add borders, pattern, laid-in, or pick-up designs as you wish. A textured handspun wool is lovely in a plain weave.

To Assemble

To find the center line, fold your woven RL in two. Mark and stay-stitch two lines, with space in between for cutting. Assemble as in diagram, sewing by hand as suggested in the section on seaming.

To Finish

Finish the warp fringes. Add fringe to the other edges if you wish. If necessary, small tucks can be taken at the shoulder for a better fit. Add whatever personal touch you wish, such as tassels, fringes, or embroidery.

3-60. Cover-up quechquemitl. Green and turquoise wool, braided bands at neck. Weaver, Phyllis Kessel. (Photograph by Kent Kammerer) (Also see detail of neck trim, Figure 5-30.)

A Cover-up Quechquemitl

Of soft wool, in deep green and light blue-green, this large quechquemitl-style shawl is an enveloping cover (Figure 3–60). It is woven in a loom pattern. Worn with points front and back, it falls nearly to the wrists. An unusual neckline trim is made of three braided strands of wool—two blue-green and one dark green—sewn to the neckline and ending in simple tassels (Figure 5–30). This treatment builds the neckline up slightly, for a very good fit. When the shawl is worn with the straight sides front and back, the trim looks a little like epaulets.

3-61. A soft mohair quechquemitl.

Mohair Shoulder Shawl

This soft, curly mohair shoulder cover is woven in a subtle block pattern of natural brown and black wools. To add to the lovely texture of the yarn, Sylvia Tacker has woven in occasional Ghiordes knots with long ends, echoing the edge fringes. Very touchable—and wearable (see Figures 3–61, 3–62, 3–63).

3-62, 3-63. The two shapes of the versatile quech-quemitl. Worn straight or pointed, by a turn around the neck. Woven by Sylvia Tacker, for Megan. (Photographs by Beverly Rush)

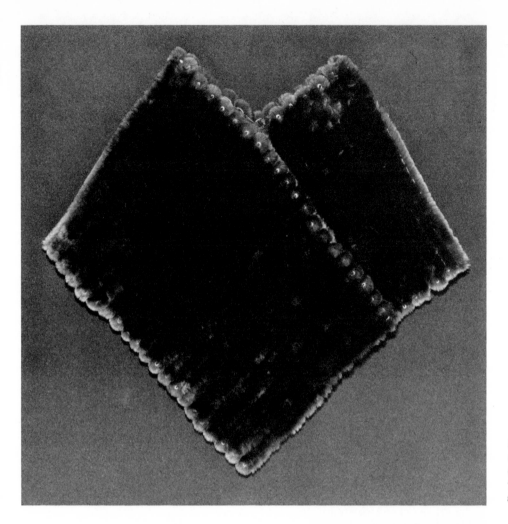

3-64, 3-65. Outside, and colorful inside of a glamorous fur quechquemitl. Double weave, fur strips and wool yarn. (Also shown in color, C-12.)

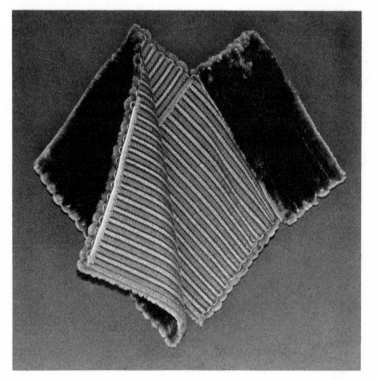

Fur and Wool Quechquemitl
Planned by weaver Hope Munn for a party-going shoulder cover, this elegant piece is beautifully detailed and woven. Strips of golden-brown fur are woven in double weave with rich wool yarns in warm orange and red-oranges. When on, it is a demure fur shawl. Opened, it is bright and striped. A zipper replaces the usual closed seam of the over-the-head version, so a party hairdo won't be disturbed. Careful turning of the fur weft creates a soft scalloped edge. Inside, meticulous hand-sewing of the zipper and seam joining makes it a complete, handsome wardrobe addition (Figures 3–64, 3–65, 3–66, and C–12).

3-66. Detail showing the hand-sewn joining on the inside of the quechquemitl. Woven by Hope Munn; shown, courtesy of Nancy Ewell. (Photographs by Beverly Rush)

Mexican Huipil-into-Jacket

A real Mexican slipover *huipil* was adapted to make a contemporary jacket (Figures 3–67, 3–68, and C–5). To minimize the change, the many-colored joining stitches were cut and removed from the center front. Yarns were matched, and the exact stitch, colors, and spacing were redone down each front edge. The seam still matches the back joining. Underarm and side seams were put in by hand to shape a sleeve, with a slit at the hemline for ease and better hang. The hem was turned up to even the bottom edge. This was not cut, in order to preserve the distinguishing sign of fabric woven on a backstrap loom—the few inches where weaving meets from the back of the loom, and from the front of the loom, is slightly looser and uneven. Inside seams were left wide with minimum cutting away.

The yoke of this *huipil* is unusual and especially rich, as the pattern was all done with wool instead of the usual cotton yarns. The bands at the neck were worked in solid, low loops. The workmanship is almost museum quality.

3-67. Mexican *huipil*-into-jacket.

3-68. Detail of richly colored wool pattern across shoulders, and the looped embroidery at the neck. Adapted by author. From La Tienda, Seattle. (Photographs by Kent Kammerer)

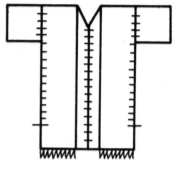

3-70. Sherpa Coat.

3-69.

TWO RECTANGLES, LONG, NARROW, WITH ADDITIONS

Sherpa Coat

From the Himalayan kingdom of Nepal comes the good-looking and practical Sherpa coat (Figures 3–70 through 3–74 and C–9). Woven of sturdy, long-wearing goat-hair yarn, these coats are the working outerwear of the Sherpas who carry loads of goods through the mountains. The easy cut allows freedom of movement. The construction, from rectangles woven on their 12″ backstrap looms, is simple and direct (Figure 3–70). Their coats are off-white goat-hair yarn with a natural gray stripe in the selvedge. Our example is woven of homespun wool, a soft medium blue with green stripes in the selvedge border (Figure C–9).

Dimensions

The characteristic Sherpa coat is a wearable, useful two-thirds length. Ours is a comfortable 30″ for a person 5′7″ tall. As the coat is made from 12″-wide lengths, you will plan for two 60″

RLs for front and back; two 20″ RLs for sleeves. The total for your warp will be 180″—approximately five yards.

To Weave

Although traditionally of plain weave, the coat may be woven in any pattern you wish. Our warp was threaded in a diamond twill so that skirt lengths could be woven with a deep design band in the contrasting green yarn. This is another bonus of planning ahead and always putting on extra warp for experimentation.

To Assemble

The narrow RLs are simply flat-seamed together. A plain, short fringe is left at the bottom, as is usual on those worn by the Sherpas.

To Finish

This coat is finished, really, when you join the seams and add the sleeves. A cuff can be turned and pressed back if you wish to have a shorter sleeve. The front opening hangs well, so no closure is needed.

3-71. Sherpa Coat. Two long rectangles, plus sleeves.

3-72. Back of Sherpa coat, to show shape, slit neck, and the back joining.

3-73. Detail of sleeve and join.

3-74. Folded Sherpa coat. Most of the handwoven coats and tunics of simple design will fold in neat squares—a boon for travelers and small storage places. Weaver, Jan Burhen. (Photographs by Kent Kammerer)

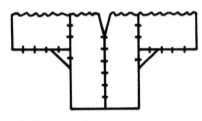

3-75. Easy Shirt.

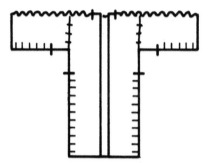

3-76. Variation of the Easy Shirt.

Easy Shirt

This garment is easy-wearing and easy to make. Two long rectangles are seamed up back and front, and an opening left for the neck. Two rectangles are added for full-length sleeves, plus a small square inserted for underarm ease (see Figures 3–75, 3–76).

Dimensions

Use your own measurements for adequate width, length, and sleeve size.

To Weave

Weave a long RL for each half of front and back —from front hem up over the shoulder and down to the back hem. Weave additional pieces for the sleeves. The small squares for the underarm can be woven with two shuttles separately. Or you can weave a RL, and then cut it in half. You can make this easement from two triangles if you prefer—either cut from a woven square, or woven to shape.

To Assemble

Match the selvedges of your two long RLs and sew a flat seam up the center front. Leave a neck slit long enough for the head to go through. Continue seaming down the back. Make a flat seam along the selvedges at the sides, sewing the easements into the sleeve and sides. Seam the sleeves.

Variation

Another way to obtain ease at the underarm is to seam the sides up to within two or three inches of the armhole. Then close the sleeve seam to within an inch or two of the armhole and leave open. We have seen jackets from Norway with an open underarm vent. They hang free and easy. If these edges are not selvedges, they will have to be finished with binding, facing, or a hem.

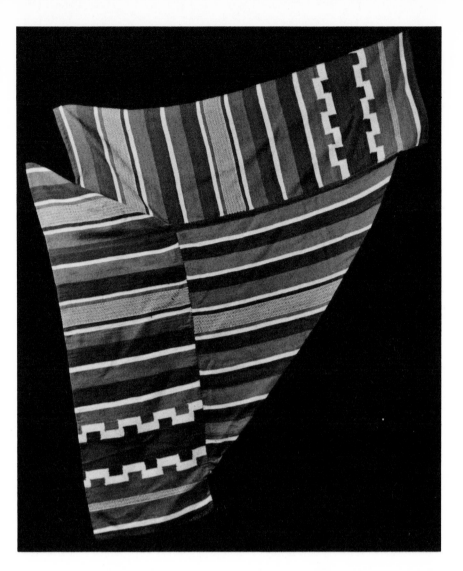

North African Man's Pants

Add a square to two long rectangles, and you have a pair of pants with plenty of striding room. These have been seen on men dancers in Morocco (Figures 1–10, 3–77, and C–16).

Two long rectangles and a square are woven in bright stripes on the same warp, wide enough for an easy fit at waist, hip, and leg. The fabric is of very fine, soft cotton, so the full center piece folds and drapes. The two RLs are joined, front and back, from waist to crotch. The square is folded and seamed to the inner edges of the leg sections. A narrow turned-back hem at the legs and waist completes the finishing. There is no drawstring or apparent way to narrow and secure the pants at the waist, but perhaps a wide girdle is wrapped around. Refer to Figure 3–77, which shows them laid out flat so that you can see the way they are put together; also see Figure C–16 for the brilliant colors.

3-77. African pants. Fine cotton, gaily striped. (Also shown in color, C-16, and Figure 1-10.) The folded square in the center gives plenty of easement for action. From La Tienda, Seattle, courtesy of Mr. and Mrs. Fred Hart. (Photograph by Kent Kammerer)

3-79. Drawstring Pants. Woven of textured black silk and finished with a short fringe. Open!

3-78.

TWO RECTANGLES, LONG, WIDE

Drawstring Pants

Astonishing, but true — two long, wide rectangles will become a pair of elegant, comfortable, drawstring pants (Figures 3–79, 3–80, 3–81). One suggestion: Unless you are *very* slim, make these of a fairly light, drapable yarn and weave. Silk or very fine wool are the best choices. Fine cotton will also be satisfactory. This simple garment has its origin in the pants worn by Mexican and Peruvian men. With variations, these full pants are found in North Africa, Guatemala, and in early times and cultures where the looms, material available, and casual fit dictated the styles.

Dimensions

Length: Measure from the waist to the desired length on the leg, add fringe or hem allowance, plus the amount needed for the drawstring tube. Width: Each RL should be 30″ wide in order to allow for fullness when the drawstring is tightened. The pants are so full, falling in folds, that they give the appearance of a skirt.

To Weave

Weave two RLs, leaving space for fringe at the end of each RL. The garment is totally simple, with no shaping, and is woven with one shuttle.

To Assemble

Fold each RL in half lengthwise. The two RLs are joined from the top down for 18″ to form the crotch. Then join the sides to form the legs. The crotch length should be quite long to allow ease of movement. A gusset may be inserted in the last 4″ of the crotch if required for comfort. Note the African pants, with a large square inset, Figure 3–77. This inset will require an additional 4″ to be woven.

To Finish

These pants fit more smoothly if they are lined with fine material cut and seamed in the same way. The lining will be stitched in at the top.

3-80. Closed! Woven by Jan Burhen. (Photograph by Kent Kammerer)

To make the drawstring tube, stitch a heading of ½″ on the machine and a ½″ to 1″ tube for the drawstrings. The tube must not be too much larger than your choice of drawstring. Leave a buttonhole slit on each side (Figure 3–81). Thread two three-yard lengths of sturdy medium-weight cord in opposite directions through the tube. One cord will start on the left, in the buttonhole, thread through the tube, and come around and out at the opposite buttonhole. Repeat with the second cord, starting at the right buttonhole.

Note: These same dimensions and finishing descriptions can be used to make a long skirt. Just seam the sides of the two RLs together, and put in the drawstring tube. This is a common usage of two rectangles and is a natural for a handwoven fabric where your creative emphasis is in the design and color of the woven cloth.

Bands and borders are effective in either the pants or the skirt. Subtle warp striping would be fun to try. Deep, fancy fringe—knotted or plain—such as that at the ends of a rebozo, would add richness and a hand-crafted look.

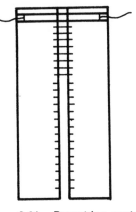

3-81. Drawstring pants.

3-82. Heavy, handspun wool "Put-over." Warm colors in loom-patterned bands. (See in color, C-7.) Woven by author. (Photograph by Beverly Rush)

Heavy Wool Put-over

The design source for this very heavy slipover top with slight sleeve shaping and a horizontal slit for the head was the Mexican *huipil* (Figures 3–82, 3–83, and C–2, C–7). We admire the patterned borders, woven or embroidered, and the warm colors used in the Mexican and Guatemalan garments, and wanted to simulate this effect with loom threading. The idea departed rapidly from the Mexican blouses after that, as it was woven on a silk warp, with weft of heavy white wool, handspun by a Northwest Indian! We chose a loom pattern that suggested the Mexican designs, threading that part of the warp in warm purple-reds and orange wool. We named it a "Put-over" partly because of its mixed origins and partly because it is so warm and loose to put over layers of sweaters or shirts for extra outdoor warmth.

Dimensions

Because of the look of it, we placed it here with wide rectangles and it can be woven this way. When put together, the warp was horizontal, so our measurements were taken from wrist to wrist, which was the length of the warp, x 2. The length was the width woven on the loom—24". It is 40" from wrist to wrist, including fringe.

To Weave

Warp was 24" in the loom for this example. The pattern warp was wool worsted; white warp was raw silk in several spins—nubby and smooth. The weft was thick, hand-spun white wool.

The selvedge was woven purposely loose for a looped-fringe effect across the shoulders and

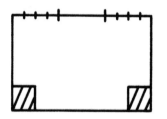

3-83.   Put-over.

bottom. Allowance was made for short warp end fringes at the sleeve ends.

To Assemble

The long woven RL was cut in half. The wide-patterned edges were matched and flat-joined along each shoulder with matching wool, with loopy selvedge as the top trim. A wide slit was left for easy-over-the-head use. Small squares were cut out to form a wide, loose sleeve, and to remove some of the bulky width around the body. These squares were not wasted—they made a perky cap! Side seams were hand sewn with white wool. The sleeves are roomy, and the wearer can tuck arms in them, or bring arms inside for a warm cocoon.

Here is one more excellent example of the timelessness of these coverings stemming from primitive loom and need. This was woven about fifteen years ago!

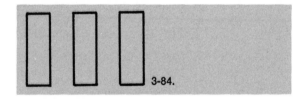

3-84.

THREE LONG RECTANGLES

The classic Mexican *huipil* (blouse or dress) is perhaps the most familiar of the clothing constructed from three rectangles (Figure C–2). In Mexico, in the different villages and groups, much variety is found in the way the patterns are used, where the embroidered, or woven, motifs are placed, and the exact method and sizes of units put together. Two wide strips may make the sides, with a narrow strip in the center. Side pieces may be narrow, forming a sleeve, and stop partway down, with a wide rectangle for the center. With so much variety, and with the subtle differences present from village to village, we suggest that you study some of the excellent material available on these garments. There is much inspiration for enrichment by woven patterns or embroidery. To generalize is difficult, but usually the different sections are joined with colorful, decorative stitches. A favorite way is to use a form of buttonhole joining, changing color every inch or two. Some garments are sewn all the way up the sides, some only part way, leaving a deep arm opening. Others are simply left open at the sides and slipped over the head like a serape. *Huipiles* vary from a short waist-length blouse to mid-calf and ankle length.

Refer to Figure C–2 for a group of these, mostly of three rectangles, but very different in patterns and ways of joining. These just hint at the varieties made.

The skirts are often long rectangles, woven on backstrap looms. They are then wrapped, pleated under sashes and belts, or otherwise secured around the waist.

Ideas to adapt to our looms and our life styles abound in *Mexican Indian Costumes* by Donald and Dorothy Cordry, University of Texas Press, Austin, Texas. They have spent a lifetime photographing, collecting, and learning to know the crafts of Mexico, and the book is an exciting source of inspiration.

3-85. The Burhenoose. Beautifully woven and fashioned long cover-up. See the rich, primitive colors, on the front cover. Woven by Jan Burhen. (Photographs by Kent Kammerer)

Burhenoose

The pattern of the "burhenoose" evolved from a desire to adapt a monk's robe or burnoose to rectangular shapes (Figures 3–85, 3–86, 3–87, 3–88, front cover). The flowing, draped garment with the simple hood is a natural for rectangular shapes. These can be woven on an 18″ to 24″ loom in sections (probably the simplest and fastest), or on a 48″ loom, weaving the entire garment at once. It could also be cut out of 2½ yards of 60″ commercially woven cloth. The pattern shown is for weaving the burhenoose in one piece on a 48″ loom.

Following are the sizes of rectangles needed if you are adapting to an 18″ loom. Refer to Figure 3–86, which shows the RL sizes. The extra 15″ length in the center panels forms the hood. The procedure for assembling these RLs is given below.

Note: If you are cutting this from 60″-wide cloth, allow seam allowance in width and cut the center front panels on the selvedge for a finished edge.

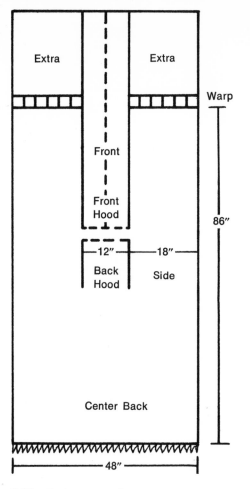

3-86. Burhenoose, plan.

If the selvedge is not attractive, use a narrow stitched hem or binding.

Dimensions for a 48″ loom: In using a wide loom, the back of the burnoose can be woven in a single width. This plus *may* not be balanced by having to weave the center front panels and sides in a three-shuttle weave, but for some the challenge is worth it! We recommend weaving the center panel 12″ wide. Then cut it in half lengthwise for the 6″ center-front RLs. This assures keeping the width exact, and it is much easier to weave three-shuttle sections than four-shuttles. Stitch the edges before cutting and cover with a buttonhole stitch.

To Weave
Refer to Figure 3–86, which shows the dimensions and weaving separations for the 48″ width. Weave up from the back hemline. The center back is woven 15″ longer for the hood. Then begin measuring for the center-front panel. At this point, it is best to mark the cloth carefully with

a double row of hand stitching across the 12″. This is easier to do while warp is under tension. Continue weaving the side panels to the length needed for back and front—86″ as in Figure 3–86. As the center panels are 30″ longer for the hood allowance, you will have extra side warp which can be left. Or weave it simultaneously into extras—two 18″ x 30″ pillows!

To Assemble
When the burhenoose comes from the loom, there are seven easy steps to assemble it:
1. Tie fringe first on all panels to prevent raveling.
2. Cut off the center-front 12″ panel between double rows of hand stitching.
3. Flat-join the top of the back hood sections together to form a 6″ V-seam in the panel. This forms the back section of the hood.
4. Make two lengths of stitching along the center line of the front panel. Cut up the center line, separating the panels.
5. Bind machine-stitched edges with needle and matching yarn in buttonhole stitch.

3-87, 3-88. Two details of the seaming in the Bur-henoose. These, in a heavy reversible purchased coat fabric. Note the selvedge used as finished edge at the front and up around the hood. By Jan Burhen.

Above
3-87. Joining at sleeve, and seam of the hood section.

6. Flat-join the center panels together on the top side. Selvedges should be on the opening edge.
7. Pin the center-front panels to the sides and hood section of the center-back panel (matching the peak of the hood), and then down to shoulder V of hood and side panel. Continue down the front side panels. Flat-join together. This joining detail is shown in Figures 3–87 and 3–88.

To Finish
The top hood seam should be covered with decorative banding or stitches. A tassel may be added in traditional monk-fashion (Figure 5–29). Decorative stitching can also be placed over the

3-88. Inside of hood, with decorative hand-sewing to cover the seam.

joining on the front panels. A closure of any kind can be used to keep center panels in place.

Variations

You may prefer sleeves to the side cape panels. This can be done simply by using the sleeve and side additions given in Figure 3–86. The dimensions will have to be changed for additional length on the side panels. The assembling process remains the same.

A reversible variation can be made by sewing two identical garments together along the outside edges, and it can be worn either side out.

4

CUT AND SEW, LOOM-SHAPING, TUBULAR WEAVE

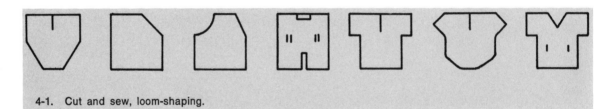

4-1. Cut and sew, loom-shaping.

Some of the favorite and most-worn garments, with roots in the simple lines and construction of primitive weavings, fit into this text, but not quite into any of the rectangle sections. We put them here in three separate groups. Some can be adapted to a more simple construction. Some will present ideas for ornamentation or enrichment in the weaving.

CUT AND SEW

White Silk Vest
While this sleeveless vest, or jacket, was cut to a pattern from handwoven yardage, we are including it because it would be possible to shape it entirely on the loom, and all edges except the hem would be selvedges (Figures 4–2, 4–3, and 4–4).

To Weave
Warp: Off-white silk and raw silk of several sizes and spins are used.
Weft: A soft, textured raw silk is used.

Weave the back up to the beginning of the armholes; then weave them to shape, on each side of the warp, up to the neckline. This could be shaped to a V, rounded, or be merely a slit. The two front sections could be woven as one; then cut, or woven, with two shuttles in two pieces.

Dimensions
Our measurements were taken to provide length enough to cover long blouses or tunics and give a good proportion over slacks. The back and two fronts were cut separately from 36″ yardage, from a size-14 commercial pattern.

To Assemble
This vest was finished like any garment cut from yardage, with a white lining fabric facing across shoulders, neck, and armholes. The facing down the fronts is 3″ of the raw silk material, folded back from selvedge, and lightly sewn down. A narrow hem turned up at the bottom is finished underneath with a decorative stitch.

To Finish
Planned to be heavily embroidered and encrusted with white stitchery, rows and rows of embroidery stitches, all in white silk and wool, are worked around the edges, at shoulder, neckline, and side seams, both front and back. A continuing embellishment project, we add a few stitches now and again between wearings. Even since these photographs were taken, another row or two have been added around the bottom and down the front. It is teamed with slacks and shirts and plain daytime dresses. And it is quite elegant over a long, long-sleeved dress for formal parties.

4-2. White raw silk vest. Embroidery stitches everywhere—edges, seams, back and front. Woven and embroidered by author.

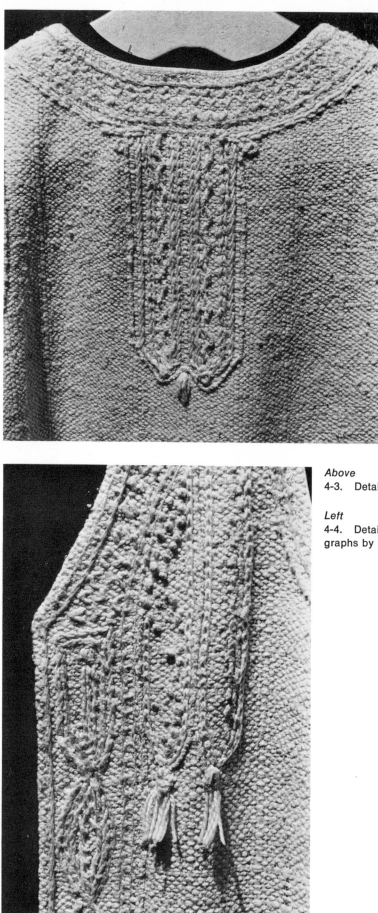

Above
4-3. Detail, back.

Left
4-4. Detail, front. (Photographs by Beverly Rush)

Left
4-5. Lila's long dress. The beautifully simple lines show off the lovely fabric.

Below
4-6. Detail of neck and sleeve banding, in plain weave. Woven by Lila Winn. (Photographs by Kent Kammerer)

Lila's Long Dress

How we wish you could see the subtle color and feel this lovely long dress! It is woven of palest celadon green yarn, two sizes, in four-harness Swedish lace threading. The banding at neck, sleeves, and hem is woven in tabby on the same warp. The simple cut shows off the beauty of the fabric (Figures 4–5 and 4–6). Lila Winn's good craftsmanship — and good taste — make this a classic of handcrafted clothing. It is fully lined with a light lining fabric and finished with a lace bordered hem.

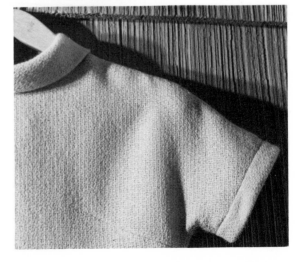

4-7. Hand-loomed cotton coat from India. Note that the sleeve is set in from the side seam like the sleeve of the African shirt, Figure 1-11. Front cut, bound, and embroidered by author.

4-8. Closure of crocheted wool and donkey beads. (Photographs by Kent Kammerer)

Coat from India

Hand-loomed from very fine cotton, with rows of thick bundles of the cotton yarn, this fabric is becoming a rather plentiful import. It is available in bedspreads and dresses. We converted a dress into a more useful coat (Figures 4–7 and 4–8). It has become one of our wardrobe stand-bys, and it is great to take or wear traveling. It folds into a neat square, and the wrinkles are minimal. Obtainable in many colors, this one is shades of turquoise, blue-green, lavender and pale yellow. We have another, in warm tones of orange, gold, and green-gold. While this coat is cut and sewn from yardage, it could be woven to shape and constructed from rectangles as described in the tunic and shirt directions.

The neckline is slightly rounded, with a narrow, stand-up collar, faced inside. We cut the dress down the center front and added a woven binding and rows of embroidery stitches. For a closure, a crocheted wool cord, with finials of turquoise donkey beads, was used.

4-9. Brushed-wool coat. Random tapestry-weave squares accent some of the stripes. (In color, C-15.)

Right
4-10. Detail. Woven by author. (Photographs by Kent Kammerer)

Orange Brushed Wool Coat

The fabric for this full-length coat was woven of bright wool worsted yarns, then teaseled and brushed to soften the colors and create a slightly fuzzy topside surface (Figures 4–9, 4–10, and C–15). Uneven stripes in the warp, an occasional weft row of a brighter orange, plus random squares of tapestry weave within some of the stripes suggest a very subtle plaid.

Dimensions

Length: It is to the dress hemline—36″ from shoulder to hem.
Width: The finished yardage is 22″ wide.

To Weave

Warp: Wool worsted in several blending warm colors—12 per inch; about 23″ in the loom for a 22″ finished width.
Weft: The same worsted as in the warp is used; one color except for random rows.

For the 36″ length, about 3½ yards were woven, leaving an extra allowance for fringe or hem.

To Cut and Assemble

No pattern was used, but some cutting and shaping were done to achieve a coat with a bit more fit than straight rectangles provide. One length is the back, with a slight tapering and rounding at shoulder and neck. Two lengths make the fronts, with the sleeve cut as one with each front panel. From the remaining pieces, the back of the sleeves and a straight piece were cut for the collar.

To Stitch

Seam the front and back sections together at the shoulder. Stitch the back sleeves to the back armholes. Stitch up the sides and underside of the sleeves.

The plain, slightly cut-out neckline was finished with a close buttonhole stitch in matching wool yarn so it could be worn without a collar. However, a collar was preferred, so it was finished on one cut edge with buttonhole stitch. The outside edge was secured with the Philippine weft-protector edge and a row of stem stitch with a short fringe sewn collar on with matching yarn.

The bottom hem was originally finished in the same way, with a 2″ fringe. Later, the fringe was cut, a ½″ hem turned up, and a row of stem stitch worked at the edge. A narrow woven band, attached at each side under the collar, ties to close the neck.

To Finish

The front edges are selvedges, but for a more finished look on this coat, they are turned back in a very narrow hem and sewn with matching wool yarn.

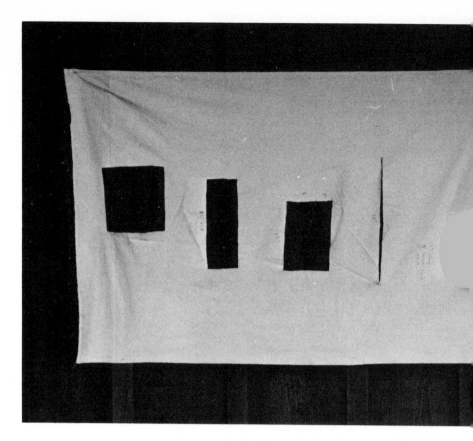

4-11. The neck banner! A variety of neck openings, shapes pinned to the side for a pattern. Dimensions lettered right on the sheet for instant try-on and reference. Devised by Jan Burhen. (Photograph by Kent Kammerer)

LOOM-SHAPED CLOTHING

The exciting and important part of planning and constructing hand-woven wearables is what the loom will help you do in weaving sections to exact size and, best of all, exact shape. The planning, measuring, and weaving may take a bit longer, but the challenge is a pleasant one, and the results are worth it. You save time at the finishing because much of the edge, hem, closures, or trim work will have been done on the loom. The parts of clothing woven in sections can be done on smaller looms, frames, or board-and-nail looms for a specific shape (see circle capes, page 100). Even if you do not have a conventional floor loom available to weave wide yardage, you can still weave and wear clothing of your own design and craftsmanship.

SPECIFICATIONS FOR LOOM-SHAPING

We have repeatedly directed you to shape a neckline during the weaving of a rectangle. Here are directions how to do this.

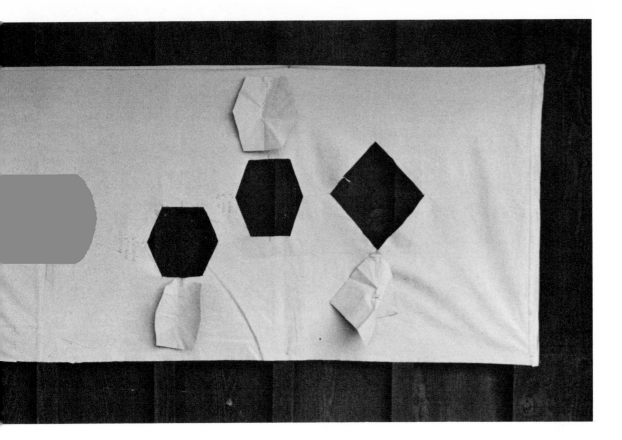

Neck Shaping

In most rectangle garments, the neck is shaped on the loom during the process of weaving. This is simply done, once the shape of the neckline is determined. As shown in the "neck banner," Figure 4–11, the exact size and shape are tried and chosen and then transferred for the loom development. The cut-out pattern may be pinned under the warp as a guide. If you prefer, measure with your tape, mark the woven web with pins for the starting width and work upward, measuring carefully as you proceed.

To Weave

It seems easier to weave the back of the neck first, so we usually suggest starting to weave at the back hem and then up to the back of the neck.

With two shuttles, weave a few rows on each side of the neck shape, leaving the neck-opening warp untouched. Then, if you want a neckline bound with a buttonhole stitch, it is best to do it at this point while the warp is under tension. When this hand-sewing is finished, proceed with two-shuttle weaving and shaping until the neck

pattern is complete. If the front of the garment is to be open, continue with two shuttles, meeting and returning from selvedge to center. In this way, you can weave the two sections at once, with a slit up the middle. The same method applies when weaving a vent at the hem, buttonholes, slits for armholes, pockets, or belt.

If you are binding the front opening with a needle stitch, it is best to do it as the weaving progresses. It will be more uniform if done under warp tension, and it will be completely finished when taken off the loom.

To Finish

The unwoven warp yarns, left in the neck opening when the weaving is removed from the loom, are cut in the center and darned back into the woven fabric. If suitable to your pattern, warps can be left as fringe.

If the opening has not been bound, tie two or more warp ends in a tight knot at the base of the weaving all around the opening. This secures the warp before darning it in, and it gives a nice firm neck edge.

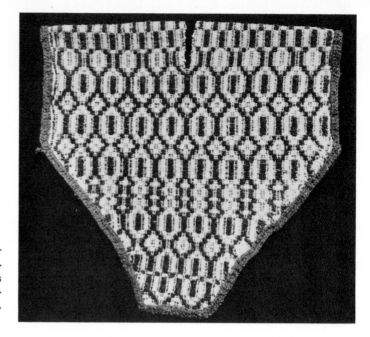

4-12. The shape of weaver Sylvia Tacker's après-ski poncho. Crochet edges. This is the back. For closure, see Figure 5-21. In color, C-11. (Photograph by Beverly Rush)

Other Shaping

These same directions apply when you are weaving a shaped armhole, or are shaping a rounded corner or part of a garment. The empty warp that is left when you weave only part of it is seldom wasted. Depending upon where it comes in the garment section, it can often be used as a warp fringe. It may come where it can be used to fashion a closing. Or it can be woven separately, along with the garment section, to use as a belt, trim, pockets, binding, or, if a large area, even a pillow. Here is where a real creative challenge enters, and you may devise some use you would not have thought of before.

For any shaped weaving, you will find it much easier and more accurate to cut a pattern. Then either place the pattern under your warp, or mark the warp so you will weave the correct shape. This is especially important when weaving a curved shape. (See Figures 4–12 and C–11.)

Sometimes the unwoven warp will become loose and sagging. This can be corrected by weaving another, separate shape simultaneously with additional shuttles, or you can weave in an occasional row of yarn—such as rug yarn—to fill the space and keep it evened up.

Use your tapestry-weaving skills. Remember that for a long, slow curve your warp and weft will have to be finer to allow for a more gradual stepping over in the rows of weaving, than for a straight-line, or angled, shape.

Shaped Poncho

For après-ski, this shaped cover-up of handspun wool, an overshot pattern in natural black, gray, and white, is very comfortable, as it does away with any bulky corners (Figures 4–12, 5–21, and C–11). Cut out a shaped pattern to follow as you weave up to the beginning of the slit for the neckhole. (Refer to remarks above about filling in unwoven warps—it will be necessary here.) The neck-slit selvedge edge is left as is, but the edges all the way around, front and back, are finished in crochet, in matching gray yarn. The simple but very effective closure detail at the front is shown in Figure 5–21.

Wide Poncho

This poncho, falling to the wrists, is a beautifully woven and finished version of an Ecuadorian poncho—the type worn by the Horse Indians of Ecuador. It is soft and warm, woven of a wool tweed yarn—forest green flecked with gold and white.

Ample warp ends were left at each end of a very wide rectangle and later plaited into perfectly done eleven-strand fringe, on both back and front. The collar is the loom-shaped section. A rectangle several inches deep, and wide enough to partially encircle the neck opening, continues into a narrowing triangle. A V-shaped neck is woven front and back. The collar piece is eased in and sewn by hand (Figures 4–13, 4–14, 4–15a, b). The edge of the roll collar is neatly finished

4-13. Wide, wonderful poncho. Styled like those from
Ecuador. Note the perfectly plaited eleven-strand fringe.

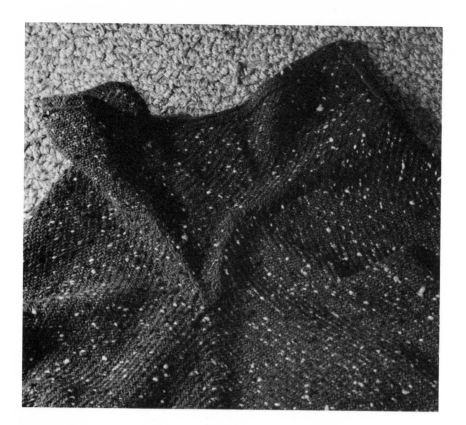

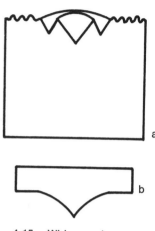

4-15. Wide poncho.

4-14. Detail of the shaped collar inset, from the inside. Woven by Lila Winn. (Photographs by Kent Kammerer)

by needle-weaving the warp ends back into the fabric. The sides are fastened at a midway point, leaving a deep armhole. The snap or button is on the inside.

Loom-shaped Tunic

Judy Thomas employs several different weaving techniques in her long tunic with woven strips for the skirt (Figure C–10). Fine wool yarns in warm golden and brown tones are used. It is woven in one piece, with no shoulder seams. The bodice, woven with a very deep, wide neckline, continues with a woven front opening. Then it goes into ankle-length panels that hang free from the waistline. Tapestry-weave patterns and color changes occur in each of the panels. The bodice is laced from the waistline to the low neckline with a cord run through two rows of brass rings. The sides are seamed from waist to armhole. The tunic is worn over a body suit, long skirt, or pants and long-sleeved shirt.

Vest, Skirt, and Belt

Paula Simmons, known for her soft and lovely Black Sheep hand-spun yarns, fashions clothing from them, as well as afghans and yardage. Her plan for weaving a vest, skirt, and belt on one warp thriftily uses all of the warp. Figure 4–16 shows the shapes.

The loom-shaped squared armhole of the vest leaves just enough unused warp to weave strips for the belt. The skirt is shaped on the loom, and long warp ends are left for a knotted fringe at the hem. The top is stitched for security and a very short fringe left, which shows above the belt, giving a nice finish. Some vests are longer than this one and some are full length. Some have the same knotted fringe as that on the skirt. All are carefully finished around the edges with crochet in blending yarn. Paula Simmons selects many shades of her natural wools for each garment, blending grays, off-whites, blacks, and browns so that they can be worn with just about any color under-dress. The vests are happily worn by both men and women.

Above
4-16. The shapes of the vest, skirt, and belt, all woven on one warp with the belt made on warps not used at arm openings. By Paula Simmons— shepherd, spinner, weaver.

Right
4-17. The vest. Note wide, easy-to-wear arm opening.

Below, left
4-18. The skirt and belt, with swingy fringe around the hemline.

Below
4-19. Back view of skirt. (Photographs by Kent Kammerer)

4-20. A-line coat, shaped on the loom, Fringed sleeve flares into a deep triangle. By spinner-weaver, Maura Shapley. (Photograph by Kent Kammerer)

A-Line Coat

Maura Shapley spun the natural gray wool weft and wove her loom-shaped coat (Figure 4–20) while still in high school. The shape is from a classic Palestinian robe. Tapering the sides from bottom to waistline and narrowing the sleeve at the upper arm make a comfortable, flattering coat with no extra bulk. The warp is a very fine, dark, gray-brown wool. Hand-spun gray weft fringe is added to give a full, two-yarn fringe for trim on sleeves and hemline. The only seams are those at the sides, from mid-sleeve to hemline. Warp ends are tied to join the wide part of the sleeve. The whole coat is shaped in the weaving, using two shuttles, on a conventional floor loom.

4-21. In the hands of weaver Luana Sever, woven wool and leather meld to form a full cape. The wool and leather form a pattern of sophisticated balance and shapes. Oive, olive-gold, dusty brown and grayed blue-greens—shown in color, C-20.

Leather and Woven Wool Cape

Wool and leather combine to make a sumptuous, imaginatively designed and crafted cape (Figures 4–21, 4–22, 4–23, and C–20). Sections of wool are woven on small, removable cardboard looms and attached to the leather sections as woven. This is a variation of the ancient Peruvian scaffold weaving. The cape carries the concept of patchwork to a very high degree of elegance. The front panels of woven wool are closed with a series of woven loops made in a continuous handcrocheted cord. Details of this ingenious closing are shown in Figures 5–18, 5–19, and 5–20.

Below
4-22. Detail of round leather insert, with wool woven to shape around it.

Right
4-23. Detail of arm slit, woven in. Close-ups of the yarn-loop closure are in Figures 5-18, 19, and 5-20. (Photographs by Beverly Rush)

Above
4-24. Another way to weave a cape. Full circle, woven on a board-and-nail-loom. Large size handspun wool, autumn-gold. Large, handcrafted buttons. Woven by Shirley Shapley.

Right
4-25. A smaller circle cape, woven on a board-and-nail-loom. Black, white, gold and rust. Heavy handspun wool weft on a black warp. Arm-slits are woven in, and buttons are large slices of deer-horn. (Photographs by Kent Kammerer)

Two Circular Capes
Two circular capes were made by a mother and her daughter (Figures 4–24, 4–25, 4–26). Board-and-nail looms were made of plywood. The weaving was accomplished by working on the floor. They report that while they were somewhat uncomfortable, the weaving went quite rapidly. Warps were added as needed as the circle widened toward the bottom.

Full Circle (Mother's)
Shirley Shapley used deep gold thick Mexican hand-spun wool (Figure 4–24). The warp is of a finer wool, tightly spun. The loom was a 9′ circle of plywood and nails.

Warp: First, the warping yarn was put over every other nail; then over the remaining nails. This provided enough warp to weave about two-thirds of the cape length. Warps were added to fill in by looping them over a row of weft. Plain weave proceeded until the hemline was reached. The woven circle was lifted off the loom, and a circle with selvedges was the result. The fronts are separated by slit weave, and the center is open, full length. The front panels lap over and are fastened by macramé loops over large pewter buttons. The arms come through the long slits at either side. By making these slits open to the bottom, there is less restraint and easier wearing.

The cape is lined, and an inner lining yoke of nylon net was inserted to help keep the shape at shoulder and neckline.

4-26. The shape of the cape. Woven by Maura Shapley. (Photograph by Kent Kammerer)

Maura's Cape

This circular cape was made on a board-and-nail loom by Maura Shapley. Black, white, orange, and gold heavy Mexican hand-spun wool was woven over a fine black wool warp (Figures 4–25 and 4–26). This cape is shorter than the full-circle one, and it is not quite a full circle. Slits were woven for armholes and buttonholes. The front just laps enough for buttoning with large antler-slice buttons.

Both of these capes fall in lovely ripples, and even though quite heavy, they hang easily from the shoulders.

Hooded Cape

Many interesting techniques and weaves are contained in this warm wool cape (Figures 4–27, 4–28, 4–29). Phyllis Kessel (the weaver whose tabards are shown in Figures 3–5, 3–6, 3–7) likes to solve weaving problems. She reports that she would do a few things a bit more easily—and differently—next time. However, the problems were solved with good results. Here we have two loom-controlled patterns—Log-Cabin in the gray and white top and hood, and Diamond Twill in the plain gray lower part, plus several shaped areas: The long piece from shoulder to shoulder, and up around the hood (Figure 4–28); the four sections, front and back, between the above strip and the body; the teardrop shape which forms the back of the hood (Figure 4–29); and the main body of the cape, which is of four sections, tapered to shape in toward the yoke.

Other special techniques include the following: Arm slits are woven in, rather high, so they are covered by the long fringe when not used. Braided fringe around the yoke is made from the warp ends of the Log-Cabin weave, using the gray and white as they fall, making a varied fringe; 3-strand, white; 4-strand, gray and white; 3-strand, gray. A crocheted band edges the hood and is worked with buttonholes for closing. The small bone buttons are suitable material, but a bit small, so she plans to replace them. Fringe around the bottom is plain warp ends, overcast to secure. Simple crochet stitch joins the side seams and center back seam in matching gray yarn and continues along each edge of the side slit at the hem. (Crochet is a good way to join for a very flat seam in a heavy wool.) The Log-Cabin blocks show up in the strip from shoulder to hood to shoulder, where the stripes are vertical and then horizontal. It fools you at casual glance into thinking that an extra square has been inserted.

This cape is a whole study in techniques. To add the final touch of complete handcraftsmanship and design, Phyllis Kessel hand-spun all the wool herself.

4-28. A skein-winder holds the cape to show the hood and yoke. One straight piece in Log-Cabin pattern (which creates some optical illusion) goes from top of shoulder, around the hood and across the other shoulder.

4-29. Detail of loom-shaped piece at back of hood, which fits into the straight strip. (Photographs by Kent Kammerer)

4-30. The flat shape of the tubular tabard. Two tubes woven for the sleeves and one for the body, with horizontal neck slit, and slits all around for the sash.

TUBULAR WEAVE

Tubular weave—weaving a tube with no side seams—works out very well for some types of clothing, when planning and measuring are carefully done. It is perfect for skirts and tunics or sheaths where you need no shaping, or where fullness is drawn in with a belt.

Gold Tabard

Exploring tubular weave, Phyllis Kessel wove a rich golden-yellow wool tabard with long sleeves (Figures 4–30, 4–31). Two sizes of tubes were woven—one for the body and one for the sleeves. The warp-ends at the hem, sleeve ends, and shoulder joinings were left in a plain short fringe for a finish. Slit weave was employed to make openings at each side, and slits were spaced around the waist for the matching woven sash

to slip through. The neck, a straight horizontal slit, was woven in, with warp ends darned in and then hemmed. Two shades and weights of the gold wool were used, which gives a slight checked appearance to the weave.

Long Tubular Skirt

The tubular-woven skirt shown in C–13 is colorful, with plain-weave tapestry details woven in some of the stripes. It is made of rayon and wool yarns, and hangs in graceful folds. The waistline band is of wrapped warp loops, with rows of colored ribbons threaded through and tied. The bottom is fringed. This skirt is a very good example of how a plain tube can be designed and woven so that it becomes a sophisticated handcrafted garment.

4-31. Warp-end fringes are at each end of the sleeve
tubes. Deep vents are woven into each side at the hem,
and a flat sash slips through the woven slits. Woven
in two shades of deep gold wool, by Phyllis Kessel.
(Photographs by Kent Kammerer)

5

ACCESSORIES, EXTRAS, SMALL STUFF

Belts, handbags, and umbrellas are all accessories that can be worn, or carried, to complement your handwoven clothing, or to enhance plain knits. All are based on geometric shapes—rectangles, squares, or triangles. We illustrate only a few, but there are lots more for you to think of and weave—scarves, other types of handbags and carryalls, hats and hoods, and many interesting belts. Try some really small things such as wristwatch bands, headbands, arm bands, and pendants.

Two Handbag Carryalls

The shoulder bag in Figure 5–2 is jute in shades of fuschia and muted red-purples. It is done in double weave, with a single-weave flap. A double row of fat, wrapped warp ends is along the bottom—the joining of the two layers of weaving. Loops, a tassel, and small wrapped tassels are added trims. The long handle is plaited and runs down the sides, ending in a plaited fringe.

Acrylic yarn is very practical for a handbag in gold and a clear red-orange, with a geometric overlay pattern (Figure 5–1). It is lined with red and expertly finished. A thick braided handle continues part way down each side, ending in step tassels. The bottom is the fold of the rectangle, and sides are hand-sewn with matching yarn.

5-1. Stepped tassels trim a rectangular handbag with overlaid pattern. Both handbags woven by Phillis Kessel. (Photographs by Kent Kammerer)

5-2. Capacious jute carryall on a long, plaited handle.

5-3. Pocket belt. Just room for a hanky or parking-meter change! Double-weave, the fine warps tie in groups, and are trimmed with square wooden beads.

Pocket Belts

The idea for these pocket belts (Figures 5–3, 5–4) came to Judy Thomas from the double-weave pocket belts worn by the Huichol men of Mexico. Her free adaptation is double-weave with pockets, woven in a straight strip. Each one is different, with variations of overlay, wrapped warp, pile weave, silhouetted tapestry weave, beads, and fringed ends which tie for the closing. All are in bright linens and warm and cool colors are combined. She calls them pocket belt/wall hangings, and these double weaves have double use.

Borrow the Huichol Indian custom of wearing several belts. First don a wide sash, then narrow belts, cords, or a pocket belt over all. They could be attached, or run through loops or slits (see Figure C–1).

5-4. Two more double-weave pocket belts, with tapestry-weave patterns. All three woven by Judy Thomas. (Photographs by Kent Kammerer)

5-5. Bright wool circles and tassels belt a slim waist.
Not showing, the foot-long warp ends which tie. Woven
by Phyllis Kessel. (Photograph by Kent Kammerer)

Tassel Belt
This bright tassel belt of circles (Figure 5–5) has
its design roots in a Peruvian technique of weaving in circles over a core. These circles are made
in the lazy-squaw basket stitch over cord. Three
full, colorful tassels tumble out of the center of
each disk. The circles are a rich red; the tassels
are deep bright red-purple, blue-purple, and blue-
green. Each unit is attached to a fat 4-strand
plaited cord, which ends in long loose ends to
tie.

5-6. Named "Wool Object" by weaver Sheila Hicks, but we suggest the idea for a waist robe or a shoulder cape. Wound warps fall from a woven band. Courtesy Craft Horizons magazine. (Photograph by Ferdinand Boesch)

Wool Object

Called a "Wool Object" by weaver Sheila Hicks, we suggest this as an idea for a shoulder or waist put-over, as an airy cape or a waist robe, or as a belt (Figure 5–6). Modified, the idea could work as a fringed waist robe or cape, with a band of weaving at the top.

A Rain of Umbrellas!

Who's for umbrellas? Now those dull black cloth ones must make way for these imaginative creations which rival the ornate parasols of the nineties.

Luana Sever brought her weaving skill, craftsmanship, and a lively imagination to umbrella coverings (Figures C–18, C–19, and 5–7 through 5–14). Most of them are combined with leather. All have areas of weaving. Each one has a different technique, design idea, and color. Triangles, shaped in the weaving, are joined to the leather sections. Colors are muted and rich. The open-weave sunshade, on the frame of a large Japanese parasol, is a nice patio accent, giving dappled shade. These umbrellas are so handsome, they would make walking in the rain a stylish pleasure!

5-7. "Rainbirds." Tan leather with handwoven camel's hair yarn, woven as yardage then cut and sewn to the leather sections. The needle-woven rainbird fringe is glued to leather backing. Appliquéd rainbirds of leather perch all around the edge.

5-8, 5-9. Outside and inside of "Rainbirds."

Right

5-10. A detail of "Blue Rainbirds." Black leather and wool sections in blues and blue-reds, woven as yardage with tapestry design. Cut and sewn to the leather sections. (Also in color, C-18.)

Below

5-11. A raindrop's view of the top. Note the yarn worked around the spike.

Left

5-12. Inside look at "Rain Moss"— a woodsy-green. Leather and wool. Wool sections are woven to shape on a cardboard loom, with scaffold-woven inserts, an ancient Peruvian technique.

Below

5-13, 5-14. Inside and outside views of "Yellow Parasol", needle-woven on the frame from a Japanese paper parasol, with mixed yarns and ribbons. A sunshine-see-through parasol, in bright yellows and yellow-greens. (In color, C-19.) All umbrellas by Luana Sever. (Photographs by Beverly Rush)

Left

5-15. Most of these are hand-crafted, of natural materials that blend with handspun yarns—Nature's colors and textures. From top left: African glass trade beads; deerhorn buttons; Mexican spindle whorl (it hardly shows, but see it on the Janus Jacket, Figure 3-57); horse bridle buttons put on with leather tie; Northwest Indian pin of copper; plaited bamboo rings for a belt, or separated for loops. On right: Woven bamboo, held on with pick; bamboo pick; deerhorn pin; loop of leather; horseshoe nails.

Right

5-16. Belt of Hungarian loom weaving encircles an enamel and copper pin; brass pick-pins; large bronze replica of a Viking pin; Danish pewter hooks; brass pin and circle; silver pin; Mexican silver pin from Taxco, shellfish shape.

CLOSURES AND TRIMS

The way a garment is fastened or trimmed is extremely important. The closure may be the main design feature, or it may be as inconspicuous as possible. When you add another material to your handwoven fabric, choose one that is right. Leather, bone, wood, or matching yarn are good with hand-spun wools and tweeds. Metals such as dull brass, copper, and pewter seem more suitable than highly polished chrome or shiny glass on handwoven fabrics. And closures should really work—not be too contrived to open and close the garment easily.

We have gathered together some that we think are appropriate, or unusual, to give you ideas of what to look for (Figures 5–15 through 5–24). Other examples are on the clothing pictured. A closure or trim made from the fabric or yarn itself is always handsome and a good choice. If it is an integral part of the fabric—made as part of the weaving—all the better. Use the many stitches of embroidery for richness and accent. Weave bands or borders with special finger techniques.

5-17. Long sash, handwoven by Marjorie DeGarmo, with folded end and tassel; pewter buttons, hooks, and ring. (Photographs by Kent Kammerer)

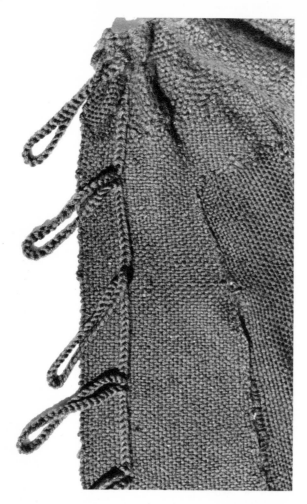

5-18. Yarn loop closure on the wool and leather scaffold-woven cape, after a closure on a Persian saddlebag. The crocheted cord is sewn down one side of the front, and out into loops.

5-19. The end of the line of loops, closed. By Luana Sever. (Photographs by Beverly Rush)

5-20. The loops are put through small slits woven on the opposite front section, then chained into each other to make a continuous, secure closing.

Left
5-21. Crochet cord, two silver Navaho buttons, repeat the curve of the pattern in the shaped poncho. Also see in color, C-11. By Sylvia Tacker. (Photograph by Beverly Rush)

Below
5-22. The Burhenoose closes with a horizontal tie of crochet, sewn on from stripe to stripe, and simply tied to close. By Jan Burhen. (Photograph by Kent Kammerer)

Left
5-23. A hand-made pick holds the Kbee Koat snugly. (Photograph by Kent Kammerer)

Above
5-24. Binding on the cut edge down the front of the coat is sewn on with rows of chain stitch; the closure is a crocheted cord of wool, with donkey beads and tiny brass bells added. By author. (Photograph by Kent Kammerer)

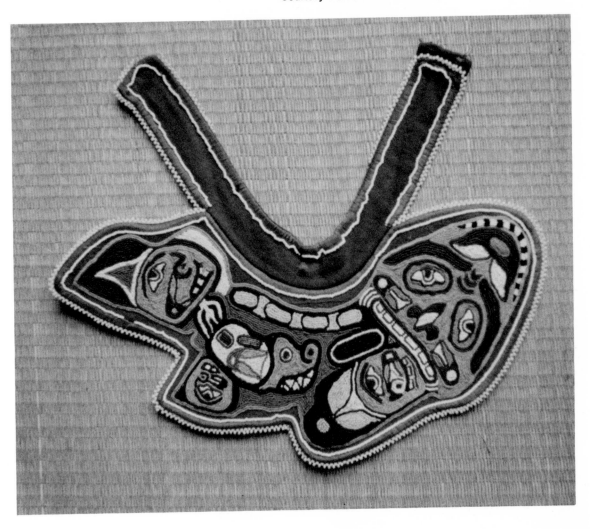

Embroidered Collar

An embroidered collar is the only trimming and a feature of a plain, long-sleeved dress of hand-loomed Irish tweed. It is done in a plain weave, of hand-spun wool, in teak brown and soft green. A Northwest Coast Indian beaded collar from the Rasmussen Collection, Portland Art Museum, was the inspiration for the irregular shape (Figure 5–25). The gift of a Danish teak and yellow-green enamel pendant helped set the shape (Figures 5–26 through 5–28). We cut paper in many trial shapes and arrived at this one, which fits the dress and the wearer.

Embroidery is done in blended shades of dull golds and olive to yellow-greens. All stitches are in circles, to complement the wood and enamel circle. The edge, worked in Palestrina stitch in a heavy, yellow-green linen thread, echoes the beading on the Indian collar.

This whole design project was fun—from inspiration to finish—and we recommend this approach to your trimmings and closures on handwoven clothing.

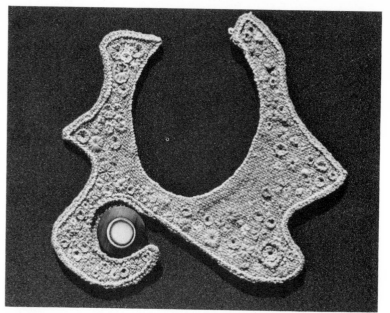

5-26. Embroidered collar on hand-loomed Irish tweed, inspired by the Northwest Indian beaded collar, Figure 5-25.

5-27. On the dress—of the same tweed.

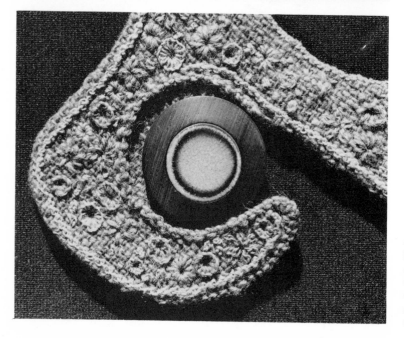

5-28. Detail, showing the bead-like Palestrina stitch around the edge. The embroidery is worked in circles, to complement the Danish teak and enamel pin. By author. (Photographs by Beverly Rush)

5-29. A heavy plaited cord is sewn along the top and back of the hood of the Burhenoose, ending in a long tassel. By Jan Burhen. (Photograph by Kent Kammerer)

5-30. Three braided cords trim the neck of the quech-quemitl, Figure 3-61. They meet, join, and end in tassels.

Yarn Trims

A braided cord covers the seam on the burnoose hood and ends in a long tassel. Rows of braided yarn and tassels form a band at the neck of a quechquemitl. These are just two of the many ways to use the fabric yarns for trim (Figures 5–29 and 5–30).

5-31. Wool tapestry-weave pocket on a wool skirt, inspired by the Mexican pocket belts. By author. (Photograph by Kent Kammerer)

POCKETS

Pockets are fun to weave. They are miniature technique showcases. There is some challenge there in weaving one exactly right for the garment and use. Not too demanding in time or materials, they are good little projects for experimenting with techniques and shapes. Somewhat expendable, not an integral part, they can be easily removed or changed. They offer a place to spark up, enrich, and add a special handwoven touch to a plain garment. And they are very handy for tucking in a hanky, or stowing your glasses.

It is interesting to speculate on the development of pockets. Primitive bags, pouches, and carrying cloths were woven and used first. Then someone, needing the use of two hands, hung the bag on a belt, or fastened it to pants or skirt. Then they were put on as a part of a garment. Often they are just for decoration and a nod to the need for a small stowing place.

Lapps use caps and tightly belted tunics for carrying pockets. Tibetans cinch up a shirt and have room for carrying things. A Mexican way is to fold up a long shirttail, tuck it in the belt, and have a handy pocket (Figure C–3). For very cold weather, wouldn't a pair of fur-lined pockets be cozy? Deep Japanese kimono sleeves are pockets. Apparently there has always been a human need to carry something along and keep it close. These are the things that are fun to experiment with and explore on your loom; that add enrichment to your handwoven garments.

Here are just two ideas—one on a wool skirt, and one on a vest (Figures 5–31, 5–32). Also see the pocket belts, Figures C–1, C–4, 5–3, and 5–4).

5-32. Tapestry-weave pocket of Irish-inspired design, for a vest of hand-loomed Irish tweed. By author. (Photograph by Kent Kammerer)

Skirt Pocket

The skirt was heavy wool, so a fairly coarse weave seemed appropriate (Figure 5–31). From a much simplified Mexican motif, and reminiscent of the Huichol pocket belt, we wove a square pocket in brilliant yellow and deep gold-brown wool. The brown was a shade darker, but matched the skirt. Technique was plain-weave tapestry with multiple dovetail color joining—much like some modern-day Mexican wool weavings. The pocket was applied with dark yarn in a buttonhole stitch. Several rows of Oriental soumak were woven across the top, in brown and yellow. To further identify with the pocket belt, two small tassels were attached at the bottom corners. Worn with a bright yellow shirt, it looked like a planned outfit.

A Vest Pocket, Loom-Shaped

This vest pocket is reminiscent of an ethnic costume— the Coptic tunic with roundels in tapestry weave (Figure 5–32).

A knee-length sleeveless vest was made of hand-loomed Irish tweed, in off-white and beige wool. To enrich it, a useful pocket was woven and attached. It was a small tapestry, designed from a stone slab in County Mayo. Yarns blended with the fabric—hand-spun medium brown wool, hand-spun wool dyed with madrona bark—a grayed orange, off-white silk, and light beige hand-spun. The techniques were plain-weave tapestry, slit weave, and Oriental soumak. The pocket was shaped to a paper pattern, and woven on a small frame loom.

A tip on applying pockets to the fabric! We allowed nearly 3″ of extra warp (white wool) along the bottom. After carefully cutting from the loom, the warp was laid in place on the fabric, and each warp end threaded through to the back. Pairs of warp were then tied together in a simple knot. No real sewing was needed. The sides were sewn in a running stitch in matching yarn, and the stitches were hidden in the weave.

123

A DEEP BOW TO THE HANDCRAFTERS

Examining, handling, and photographing the handwoven clothing shown in this book, we have been aware of fine finishing details that can't be appreciated in a photograph. The feel and good looks of the beautiful fabrics are a pleasure. They have been carefully woven and properly finished for beauty and wear. Some niceties of detail that we noted:

Small monograms hand-embroidered inside

All seams hand-finished with matching yarn; sometimes with an embroidery stitch

Delicate lace on the hem of a dress lining

Hemstitching on the loom where an opening is woven to prepare a heading for warps woven back in

An embroidered flower on the lining where a button is sewn on

Hand-sewing wherever possible

Covering a machine-stitched seam with hand sewing

Professional, sophisticated finishing such as facings and nylon net, reinforcing for wear and fit

All of these craftsmanly touches add to the joys of creating handwovens. Our modern-day weavers measure up—and then some! Admiring thanks to each of you whose handwovens appear in this book.

AN APPROPRIATE CLOSURE

We hope you have found in the doing and the wearing some challenging weaving ideas—and some fun; more awareness of the craftsmanship of the early weavers and their ability to adapt materials and tools to needs; and more awareness of natural fibers, their preparation, and their use in weaving garments that retain a carefully handcrafted look; that reflect planning, good workmanship, and design.

We hope you have enriched your craft experiences and have found some real favorites in our selection.

INDEX